TOP GRAMMAR

For Beginners

초급 - 2

WorldCom

1. Forms

문법을 제대로 습득하기 위해서는 일정한 뜻을 나타내는 형식을 정확히 익혀야만 합니다. 특히 정확한 형태 습득은 문법 학습의 초기와 완성 단계에서 중요하기 때문에, 각 unit의 핵심적인 형태를 예문과 함께 제시했습니다. 예습과 복습용으로 활용합시다.

2. Meaning & Use

일정한 문법 형태가 어떤 뜻으로 어떻게 쓰이는지를 친절하게 설명했습니다. 단순한 암기가 아니라 이해를 통해 문법을 제대로 익힐 수 있도록 했습니다.

3. Key point

학교 내신시험, TOEIC Bridge, TOEIC, TEPS 등 주요 영어시험에 자주 출제되는 사항을 쉽게 이해할 수 있도록 설명했습니다. 꼼꼼히 익혀서 특목고 진학 등의 꿈을 이루는 바탕을 마련합시다.

4. Exercises

학교 내신시험이나 TOEIC 등 다양한 시험에 충분히 대비할 수 있도록 정밀하게 문제를 구성했습니다. 또한 문제 풀이를 통해 자연스러운 문법을 구사할 수 있도록 배려했으니 한 문제, 한 문제를 철저하게 익힙시다.

5. Chapter Review

각 chapter에서 학습한 사항을 완전히 자신의 것으로 만들 수 있도록 보다 다양한 유형과 활용도가 높은 예문으로 문제를 구성했습니다. 자신의 문법 실력을 한 차원 높이는 계기로 활용합시다.

이와 같은 과정을 통해 자연스럽고 정확한 영어를 구사할 수 있게 될 뿐만 아니라, TEPS 등 주요 영어시험에 완벽하게 대비할 수 있습니다. 차분히 과정을 밟아나갑시다.

수많은 영문법 교재가 출간되었음에도 불구하고 학생들의 문법 실력을 체계적이고 효율적으로 길러 주는 책을 찾기가 몹시도 어려운 실정입니다. 활용도가 현저히 떨어지는 사항을 자세하게 다루어 불필요하게 부담을 가중시키거나 다양한 영어 시험에 대비해야 하는 우리 학생들의 실정에 걸맞지 않는 사항에 치중하는 교재들이 흔합니다. 또한 학생들이 제대로 된 영어 실력을 갖출 수 있게 배려한 영문법 교재도 찾아보기 어렵습니다.

'Top Grammar는 이와 같은 현실을 개선하기 위한 오랜 노력의 결과로 탄생한 문법 교재입니다. "조동사 used to의 부정형"과 같이 문법학자나 관심을 가질 만한 불필요한 사항은 과감히 배제하고 꼭 필요한 문법 사항을 체계적으로 이해할 수 있도록 배려했습니다. 또한 활용도가 높고 흥미로운 예문을 선택함으로써 본 교재의 학습을 통해 자연스럽게 영어 실력을 향상시킬 수 있도록 했습니다. 마지막으로 학교 내신시험 등 영문법 지식이 활용되는 모든 시험들에서 빈번하게 출제되는 사항을 깔끔하게 정리했습니다.

문법이란 뜻을 자연스럽게 구성하기 위한 약속입니다. 따라서 뜻과 모양, 그리고 쓰임새 사이의 유기적인 관계를 체계적으로 이해해야만 제대로 된 문법 실력, 더 나아가서, 영어 실력을 기를 수 있습니다. 이와 같은 점을 감안한 Top Grammar는 정말로 꼭 필요한 내용을 단기간내에 효율적으로 학습할 수 있도록 하나하나의 설명과 하나하나의 예문을 세심하게 배려한 최고의 문법서입니다. Top Grammar의 체계적인 문법 프로그램을 통해 진정한 문법 실력과 영어 실력을 기를 수 있게 되기를 간절히 기원합니다.

Practical English

모든 영문법 사항들이 일상적으로 빈번하게 쓰이지는 않는다. 원어민마저도 평생에 한 번도 쓰지 않는 문법 사항들도 많이 있다. TOP GRAMMAR는 일상적으로 빈번하게 쓰이는 실용적인 문법 사항들을 체계적으로 편성했다.

Living Grammar

자연스럽게 쓰이는 문장을 통해서야 비로소 문법은 생명력을 얻는다. 실제 용례(usage)가 뒷받침이 되지 않으면 문법은 생명을 잃고 만다. 이와 같은 점을 고려하여 TOP GRAMMAR는 원어민들이 자연스럽게 구사하는 예문을 중심으로 편성했다. 이처럼 "살아 있는 문법"을 학습해야만 탄탄한 문법 실력을 배양할 수 있을 뿐만 아니라 자연스러운 영어 구사력을 기를 수 있기 때문이다. TOP GRAMMAR의 생명력이 강한 예문을 통해 영어다운 영어를 구사할 수 있도록 하자.

Useful Language

학교 내신시험, 수능, TOEIC Bridge, TOEIC, TEPS 등 주요 영어시험에서는 여전히 문법의 비중이 상당하다. 이들 시험에서는 활용도가 높은 문법 사항들이 주로 출제되는데, TOP GRAMMAR는 이와 같은 빈출 사항들을 짜임새 있게 정리했다. 또한 TOEFL iBT의 Speaking과 Writing 영역에 활용될 수 있는 주요 사항들도 본문에서 다루었기 때문에, TOP GRAMMAR로 각종 영어시험의 문법 영역에 완벽히 대비할 수 있다.

American English

영국식 영어(British English)와 미국식 영어(American English)는 발음, 철자, 표현, 일부 문법 사항 등에서 다양한 차이를 나타낸다. 우리나라 학생의 경우는 초등학교부터 고등학교까지 미국식 영어로 학습을 하기 때문에 미국식 영어를 정확히 익히는 것이 올바른 순서이다. 학교 내신시험이나 수능 시험, 그리고 TOEFL iBT나 TEPS는 철저하게 미국식 영어를 측정한다. 반면 TOEIC의 경우는 발음에서만 일정 정도 영국식 영어를 채택했지만 독해나 문법은 완전히 미국식 영어를 측정한다. 따라서 우리나라 학생들은 무엇보다도 미국식 영어를 제대로 습득하는 것이 우선 순위이다. 이와 같은 점을 고려하여 TOP GRAMMAR는 철저하게 미국식 영어를 채택했다.

Engaging Learning Activities

문법 실력은 현실감 있는 상황에서 실제로 자연스러운 문법을 구사하는 연습을 통해서만 제대로 길러질 수 있다. 따라서 문법 문제 하나하나가 일상적인 상황에서 활용될 수 있는 능력을 측정하거나 학생의 흥미를 끌 수 있는 활동으로 구성되어야 한다. TOP GRAMMAR는 자연스러우면서도 흥미로운 예문과 다양한 문제 유형을 통해 학생들이 보다 쉽고 편안하게 문법에 다가갈 수 있도록 자상하게 배려했다. 또한 자연스러운 맥락에서 활용될 수 있는 문장들을 예문으로 선택함으로써 학생들이 일정한 문법 형태가 실제로 쓰이는 맥락(context)을 이해할 수 있게 했다. 따라서 TOP GRAMMAR를 학습함으로써 진정한 영어 실력을 흥미롭게 또한 체계적으로 기를 수 있다.

Contents

Chapter 9

비교

Form

	동사(+not)	as	형용사	as	
Ann	is isn't	as	old tall clever	as	Tom.

	동사(+not)	as	부 사	as	
Ann	runs doesn't run	as	fast quickly slowly	as	Tom.

Meaning & Use

1_ 비교는 둘 이상의 사람이나 사물의 차이를 나타내는 표현을 말한다.

2_ 형용사나 부사의 원래의 형태인 원급을 사용하는 동등 비교는 「as+형용사/부사+as」의 형식으로 쓰이며 '~만큼 ~하다' 의 뜻을 나타낸다.

Tom is as old as Jane.

Jean sings as well as Tim.

3_ 동등 비교의 부정은 「not as[so]+형용사/부사+as」로 '~만큼 ~하지 않다' 의 뜻을 나타낸다.

My computer is not as fast as Donna's.

Ann doesn't study as hard as Diana.

Key point _ less + 원급 + than

TEPS 등의 시험에는 "~만큼 ~하지 않다" 라는 뜻을 나타내는 "less 원급 than"을 때때로 출제한다. 이 구문에서 less 다음에 비교급 형태인 ~er을 쓰지 않도록 특히 주의해야 한다.

Aristotle is less great than Plato. (O)

Aristotle is less greater than Plato. (X)

Exercises

A Sue와 Tom에 대한 사항을 보고 as ~ as 또는 not as ~ as를 사용하여 주어진 문장을 완성하시오.

	Age	Weight	Height	Reading	Getting up	Exercise
Sue	14	40kg	1.60m	2 pages/min	6:40	Mon, Fri
Tom	15	43kg	1.60m	3 pages/min	6:10	Mon, Fri

1 Sue (be, old) _________________________________ Tom.

2 Sue (be, heavy) _______________________________ Tom.

3 Sue (be, tall) ________________________________ Tom.

4 Sue (read, fast) ______________________________ Tom.

5 Sue (get up, early) ____________________________ Tom.

6 Sue (exercise, often) __________________________ Tom.

B 1, 2번의 예와 같이 as ~ as 또는 not as ~ as를 사용하여 문장을 만드시오.

1 fall / hot / summer
   Fall is not as hot as summer.

2 Peter (15) / old / Sam (15)
   Peter is as old as Sam.

3 horses / big / elephants
   ____

4 bikes / run / fast / cars
   ____

5 spring / cold / winter
   ____

6 Chris (50kg) / heavy / Holly (50kg)
   ____

7 monkeys / clever / people
   ____

Unit 02 — 비교급

Form			
	형용사 비교급	than	
Mary is	**taller**	**than**	I.
	more beautiful		
	부사 비교급	than	
Jack worked	**harder**	**than**	I.
	more quickly		

Meaning & Use

1_ 두 대상을 비교하여 '~보다 더 ~하다' 라는 의미를 나타내기 위해 「비교급+than」의 형식을 쓴다.

Sue is older than me.

Judy works harder than Tom.

2_ 「비교급+than」은 「not as ~ as」로 바꾸어 나타낼 수 있다.

Joan is taller than Jim. = Jim isn't as tall as Joan.

Albert runs faster than Dave. = Dave doesn't run as fast as Albert.

3_ 비교급을 만드는 규칙은 다음과 같다.

- 1음절의 형용사나 부사는 -er을 붙인다.

    old – older, tall – taller, fast – faster, hard – harder

- 「단모음+단자음」으로 끝나는 1음절 형용사는 자음을 한번 더 쓰고 -er을 붙인다.

    hot – hotter, big – bigger, fat – fatter, thin – thinner

- -e로 끝난 1음절 형용사와 부사는 -r만 붙인다.

    wide – wider, large – larger, late – later

- -y로 끝나는 형용사는 -y를 -i로 바꾸고 -er을 붙인다.

    easy – easier, busy – busier, happy – happier

- 2음절 이상의 형용사나 부사는 앞에 more를 쓴다.

    beautiful – more beautiful, interesting – more interesting   예외) early – earlier

- 불규칙으로 변하는 형용사와 부사가 있다.

    good/well – better, bad/badly – worse, many/much – more, little – less

Exercises

A 다음 형용사와 부사의 비교급을 쓰시오.

1 big _______________ 2 easy _______________

3 thin _______________ 4 interesting _______________

5 expensive _______________ 6 large _______________

7 early _______________ 8 good/well _______________

B 다음 비교급 형용사와 부사의 원급을 쓰시오.

1 later _______________ 2 worse _______________

3 hotter _______________ 4 happier _______________

5 more _______________ 6 wider _______________

7 busier _______________ 8 fatter _______________

C 비교급을 써서 다음 문장을 완성하시오.

1 A bicycle is (cheap) _______________ a motorcycle.

2 A car goes (fast) _______________ a bike.

3 A computer is (good) _______________ a typewriter.

4 A cell phone is (convenient) _______________ a telephone.

5 New York summers are (hot) _______________ summers in London.

6 Karen is (heavy) _______________ Judy.

7 Color printers are (expensive) _______________ black-and-white printers.

8 A village is (small) _______________ a town.

9 A cat is (big) _______________ a rat.

10 Old shoes are (comfortable) _______________ new ones.

11 The new school is (bad) _______________ the old one.

12 Music is (interesting) _______________ math.

13 My father came home (late) _______________ my brother.

14 New cell phones are (thin) _______________ old ones.

15 A train is (safe) _______________ a bus.

Form

	the + most + 형용사/부사	
Mt. Everest is	**the highest**	mountain in the world.
	the most beautiful	
Susan works	**(the) fastest**	of all the workers.
	(the) most happily	

Meaning & Use

1_ 셋 이상의 대상을 비교할 때는 최상급을 쓴다. 최상급은 '가장 ~하다' 의 뜻을 나타내며 형용사나 부사에 -est나 most를 붙여 만든다.

	원급	비교급	최상급
형용사	tall	taller	**tallest**
	big	bigger	**biggest**
	busy	busier	**busiest**
	beautiful	more beautiful	**most beautiful**
부사	hard	harder	**hardest**
	early	earlier	**earliest**
	hungrily	more hungrily	**most hungrily**
불규칙 형용사 / 부사	good/well	better	**best**
	bad/badly	worse	**worst**
	many/much	more	**most**
	little	less	**least**

2_ 최상급 표현은 「the+형용사/부사+-est」 또는 「the+most+형용사/부사」 라는 형식으로 나타내는데, 부사의 최상급 앞의 the는 생략할 수 있다. 비교 범위를 나타낼 때, in 다음에는 소속 집단이 of 다음에는 비교의 대상들이 오는 것이 보통이다.

Ann studies (the) hardest in the class.

Judy is the youngest of the students.

Jack works (the) fastest of all the workers.

A 주어진 문장의 시작 부분과 나머지 부분을 연결하여 문장을 완성하시오.

		B	C
1	My grandma is ( ) ( )	A. the largest country	a. in the orchestra.
2	Alfred is ( ) ( )	B. the longest river	b. in my family.
3	Seoul is ( ) ( )	C. the best musician	c. in Korea.
4	Russia is ( ) ( )	D. the best worker	d. in the group.
5	The pianist is ( ) ( )	E. the biggest city	e. in America.
6	The Missouri River is ( ) ( )	F. the oldest woman	f. in the world.
7	My room is ( ) ( )	G. the most expensive	g. of the five girls.
8	The BMW is ( ) ( )	H. the youngest	h. of the three rooms.
9	Sue is ( ) ( )	I. the smallest	i. of the ten cars.

B 다음 그림을 보고 문장을 완성하시오.

1 Dave is as tall as ______________.

2 Ann is older than ______________.

3 Sue is taller than ______________.

4 ______________ is the youngest and ______________ is the oldest.

5 ______________ is the heaviest and ______________ is the lightest.

6 ______________ is the shortest.

A 잘못된 부분을 바르게 고치시오.

1 Tim is more older than Jane.

2 The Nile is longest river in the world.

3 He is younger as his wife.

4 Seoul is the larger city in Korea.

5 I think San Francisco is the more beautiful city in the United States.

6 New York is biger than Los Angeles.

7 I think Japanese is easyer than English.

8 I speak English more better than my friends.

9 Susan is the most prettiest girl in the class.

10 Antonio gets up the most early.

11 The restaurant is the goodest in our town.

12 My grades are badder than yours.

13 Diana runs the faster than Mike.

14 Yesterday was more hot than today.

15 I think Mexican food is a most delicious.

16 Jenny is the better writer in the class.

17 Autumn Farm is the most widest road in the area.

B 알맞은 것을 고르시오.

1 What's (the longest / longer than) river in the world?

2 Alfred is (the brightest / brighter than) of all the students.

3 George is (the most diligent / more diligent than) student in the class.

4 Yesterday was (the worst / worse than) last Monday.

5 Our Korean teacher speaks (the most quickly / more quickly than) of all the teachers.

6 The first movie was (the funniest / funnier than) the second one.

C 주어진 단어의 비교급 또는 최상급을 사용하여 대화를 완성하시오.

1 A: How old is Ann? Is she your _____________ (old) child?

B: No, she's the middle child of three. She's _____________ (young) than Jack but _____________ (old) than Kate.

2 A: Who's the _____________ (tall) of you all?

B: Well, Jill is _____________ (short) than Erica, and Erica is _____________ (tall) than any other girl.

3 A: What's the _____________ (fast) animal in the world?

B: Well, the lion is _____________ (slow) than the cheetah, and the cheetah is _____________ (fast) than any other animal.

D 주어진 형용사를 사용하여 최상급 문장과 비교급 문장을 만드시오.

1 a bus / an airplane / a train (fast)

An airplane is the fastest of the three.

An airplane is faster than a train. or A train is faster than a bus.

2 a golf ball / a football / a baseball (large)

3 an elephant / a chimpanzee / a rabbit (heavy)

4 a monkey / a dog / a turtle (smart)

5 a year / a month / a week (long)

E 다음 밑줄 친 부분에 가장 적절한 것을 고르시오.

1 Dogs are ___________ cats.
- a. friendlier than
- b. friendly than
- c. as friendlier as
- d. more friendly

2 Mary's car is ___________ Jane's.
- a. expensive than
- b. more expensive than
- c. more expensive
- d. expensiver than

3 A: Let's go to the Oak Restaurant.
  B: No, let's not. It's ___________ restaurant in town!
- a. worst
- b. the best
- c. best
- d. the worst

4 A: Which is better, the big computer or the small one?
  B: The small one is too slow. It's ___________ the big one.
- a. better than
- b. worse
- c. worse than
- d. badder than

5 Mt. Everest is ___________ Mt. Kilimanjaro.
- a. higher than
- b. tall than
- c. high than
- d. higher as

6 The Pacific is ___________ ocean in the world.
- a. bigger
- b. the big
- c. the biggest
- d. the most big

7 Susan is ___________ Jack.
- a. more carefuller
- b. careful as
- c. more careful than
- d. careful than

8 The Korean language is ___________ subject in school.
- a. easiest
- b. the easiest
- c. the easier
- d. easier than

9 Whales are ___________ rabbits.
- a. more heavier than
- b. heavier
- c. heavier than
- d. heavy than

10 Apples are ___________ candy.
- a. more sweet than
- b. not as sweet as
- c. not more sweeter than
- d. sweet as

11 Mary is ___________ actress in the world.
    a. more beautiful   b. beautifulest
    c. the most beautifulest   d. the most beautiful

12 Jane is ___________ Lora.
    a. as much tall as   b. as tall than
    c. as tall as   d. as taller as

13 This question is ___________ than any other question.
    a. the more difficult   b. more difficult
    c. most difficult   d. more difficulter

14 The red building is ___________ in the city.
    a. the most oldest   b. the oldest
    c. oldest   d. most oldest

15 A sofa is ___________ than a chair.
    a. more comfortably   b. comfortabler
    c. the more comfortable   d. more comfortable

16 Angela is a ___________ her sister.
    a. better student than   b. better student as
    c. gooder student than   d. best student

17 Greg drives ___________ than his brother.
    a. more careful   b. more carefully
    c. careful   d. the more carefully

18 Farmers get up ___________ other people.
    a. the earliest   b. more early than
    c. earlier than   d. more earlier than

19 Lisa is ___________ student in the class.
    a. the most beautiful   b. the more beautiful
    c. most beautiful   d. the best beautiful

20 Let's take his car. It's ___________ mine.
    a. the more bigger than   b. the most biggest
    c. bigger than   d. more bigger than

Chapter 10

조동사

조동사의 기본 개념

Form

1 I **can** swim well.

2 He **must** be a teacher.

3 **Can** you help me?

Meaning & Use

1_ 조동사는 동사의 한 종류로서 동사와 함께 쓰여 그 동사를 도와주는 역할을 한다. 조동사와 함께 쓰이는 동사를 본동사라고 하며, 조동사는 본동사와 함께 능력, 허락, 추측, 의무, 충고, 부탁 등의 의미를 나타내는데, 주요 조동사로는 can/could, may/might, will/would, should, must 등이 있다.

2_ 조동사는 다음과 같은 특징을 지닌다.
- 인칭이나 수에 따라 모양이 바뀌지 않는다.
  I can do it. He can do it, too.
- 조동사 뒤에는 동사원형이 온다.
  He must go there now.
- 부정문, 의문문에 do를 쓰지 않는다.
  "May I go home now?" "No, you may not."

3_ 조동사의 부정은 조동사 뒤에 not을 쓰며, 보통 축약 형태로 will not은 won't, should not은 shouldn't, must not은 mustn't처럼 쓰인다. 특히, can의 부정형은 cannot 또는 can't 임에 유의해야 한다.
I cannot (= can't) do it myself.

4_ 조동사의 의문문은 조동사와 주어를 바꾸어 「조동사+주어+동사원형 ~?」과 같이 만든다. 응답은 「Yes, 주어+조동사」또는 「No, 주어+조동사+not」으로 한다.
"May I go out?" "Yes, you may." / "No, you may not."

A   적절한 것을 고르시오.

1   Can he (play / plays) the guitar?

2   Could you (pass / passed) the salt, please?

3   Peter didn't get my call last night. He must (be / was) out of town.

4   Chris (may / mays) be here on the weekend.

5   I couldn't (go / went) to the party because I was too busy.

B   밑줄 친 부분에 필요하면 -(e)s를 붙이고 필요하지 않으면 X표 하시오.

1   Ann <u>play</u>___ Ping-Pong at the gym every weekend.

2   Bill <u>can</u>___ solve the problem by himself.

3   It's cloudy. It <u>may</u>___ rain tonight.

4   She <u>must</u>___ clean her room now.

5   Jack <u>should</u>___ care for her mother.

C   다음 문장을 부정문으로 고쳐 쓰시오. 조동사는 축약하시오.

1   Ann can speak Chinese.

   ____

2   Mary must wash her clothes now.

   ____

3   Romeo must die.

   ____

4   You should play computer games every day.

   ____

5   Juliet will get the best grade in the test.

   ____

Form

주어	can(not)	동사원형		주어	could (not)	동사원형	
I/You	**can**			I/You	**could**		
He/She	**cannot**	**speak**	English.	He/She	**could not**	**speak**	English.
We/They	**can't**			We/They	**couldn't**		

Can/Could	주어	동사원형	Yes,	주어	can	No,	주어	can't/couldn't
Can **Could**	you he they	**swim?**	Yes,	I he they	**can.** **could.**	No,	I he they	**can't.** **couldn't.**

Meaning & Use

1_ can은 '~할 수 있다' 의 뜻으로 현재나 미래의 능력 또는 가능을 나타낸다.

I can play the viola.

We can go on a picnic next Friday.

2_ can의 부정은 cannot이며 일상적으로는 can't로 축약하여 쓴다.

Erica cannot come to the party tonight.

Judy can't play the cello.

3_ 과거의 능력을 나타낼 때는 can의 과거형인 could를 쓴다.

I could finish my homework on time.

I couldn't remember your telephone number yesterday.

4_ can/could 대신에 be able to를 쓸 수 있다. 일상적으로는 can/could가 더 많이 쓰이지만 can의 미래형으로는 will be able to를 써야 한다.

They are able to (= can) have a baby.

I was able to (= could) solve the math problems by myself.

I'll be able to drive next year.

A 문맥에 적절한 것을 고르시오.

1 George (can't / couldn't) play with us yesterday.

2 (Can / Could) you play the piano as a child?

3 I can read Japanese, but I (can't / couldn't) speak it.

4 I'm sorry, but I (can't / couldn't) hear you. It's too noisy here.

5 Your cell phone wasn't working yesterday. I (can't / couldn't) leave a message.

B 주어진 단어와 can을 사용하여 문장을 만들고 짧게 답하시오.

1 David / drive / his father's car

_______________________________________? Yes, _______________________.

2 Julie / the guitar / play

_______________________________________? No, _______________________.

3 draw / you / beautiful pictures

_______________________________________? No, _______________________.

4 Susie / ride / a bicycle

_______________________________________? Yes, _______________________.

5 type / Philip / 50 words a minute

_______________________________________? No, _______________________.

C be able to의 적절한 형태로 문장을 완성하시오..

1 The baby _______________ walk and talk soon.

2 I tried very hard and _______________ solve all the math problems.

3 My father _______________ open the door without the key.

4 I _______________ find the answer.

5 Monkeys _______________ walk on two feet.

Form

주어	조동사	동사원형	
You	can	sit	here.
	may		

주어	조동사 + not	동사원형	
You	cannot/can't	sit	here.
	may not		

조동사	주어	동사원형	
Can	I	wait	here?
Could	we		
May			

Yes,	주어	조동사
Yes,	you	can.
		may.

No,	주어	조동사 + not
No,	you	cannot.
		can't.
		may not.

Meaning & Use

1 _ can과 could는 능력 이외에 허락을 나타낼 수 있다. 이 경우 could는 과거의 의미를 지니지 않는다.

"Can I use your phone?" "Yes, of course."

"Could I ask you a favor?" "Yes, certainly."

2 _ may도 허락의 의미를 나타낸다. could가 can보다 정중한 표현이고, may는 격식을 갖춘 표현이다.

"May I use your computer?" "Yes, you may."

"May I come in?" "No, you may not."

3 _ 허락을 구할 때는 흔히 please와 함께 쓴다. please는 주어 바로 뒤나 문장 끝에 둔다.

Could I borrow your car, please?

May I please use your pen?

Key point _ may as well

TEPS 등의 시험에서는 「~하는 편이 더 낫다」라는 뜻의 「may as well ~」을 종종 출제한다. 이때 ~에 반드시 동사원형이 와야 함을 꼭 기억하자.

You may as well laugh at your mistakes. (O)

You may as well to laugh at your mistakes. (X)

A 1번처럼 허락을 구하는 Can I ~? 또는 Could I ~? 표현으로 고치시오.

1 I want a glass of water. (have) _Can/Could I have a glass of water, (please)_?

2 I want to use your pen. (use) _______________________?

3 I want some more coffee. (have) _______________________?

4 I want to leave early tomorrow. (leave) _______________________?

5 I want to take your picture. (take) _______________________?

6 I want to borrow your car. (borrow) _______________________?

B 주어진 표현을 사용하여 대화를 완성하시오.

May I close the window?	May I sit here?
Can I pay by credit card?	Can I bring my friends?
Can I speak to the doctor?	Can I watch it?

1 A: I'm cold. _______________________
   B: Yes, you may.

2 A: This bag is $30.
   B: _______________________
   A: Sure.

3 A: There's a good show on TV at 8:00. _______________________
   B: No, you can't. Prepare for tomorrow's test.

4 A: _______________________
   B: Sure. The seat is not taken.

5 A: Please come to my party next Saturday.
   B: _______________________
   A: Of course.

6 A: Hello. Dr. White's office. This is Mary speaking.
   B: Hello. This is David Smith. _______________________
   A: I'm sorry, but he went out for lunch.

요청을 나타내는 will, can, would, could

Form

조동사	주어	동사원형		긍정 응답	부정 응답
Can				Yes, of course.	
Could	you	**close**	the door?	Certainly. Sure.	I'm sorry, but I can't ...
Will				OK.	I'd like to, but ...
Would				I'd be glad to.	

Meaning & Use

1 _ 상대방에게 뭔가를 요청할 때 Can, Could, Will, Would ~?를 쓴다. can, will보다는 could, would가 보다 격식을 차린 표현이다.

Can/Will you come to the party?

Could/Would you send the report?

2 _ 보다 더 정중한 요청을 할 때 could, would와 함께 please를 쓴다. please는 허락을 구하는 경우와 같이 주어 바로 뒤나 문장 끝에 쓴다.

Would you please sign this form?

Could you close the door, please?

3 _ 긍정적인 응답은 Yes, of course., Certainly., Sure., OK., I'd be glad to. 등을, 부정적인 응답은 I'm sorry, but I can't., I'd like to, but ...등의 표현을 사용한다.

"Can you wait here for a minute?" "Sure."

"Would you mail this for me?" "I'd like to, but I don't have time."

Key point _ **Would you mind ...?**

학교 내신시험에서는 요청을 나타내는 Would you mind ...?에 대한 응답을 자주 출제한다. 이 경우 "No, not at all."이라고 응답해야 요청을 들어주겠다는 뜻이 됨을 명심하자.

"Would you mind opening the window?" — "No, not at all."

Exercises

A   Ann과 Julie의 대화에 적절한 응답을 고르시오.

1   Julie: Would you please drive me to class today?

Ann: (Yes, I wouldn't. / I'd be glad to.)

2   Julie: Can you lend me five dollars?

Ann: (Sure. / No, I will.)

3   Julie: Can you take this book back to the library for me? I'm late.

Ann: (Sure. / No, I can.)

4   Julie: Could you close the window? I'm cold.

Ann: (Yes, I couldn't. / Certainly.)

5   Julie: Can you turn the radio down? I have a math quiz this morning.

Ann: (Sure. / No, I can.)

6   Julie: Will you pick up some milk at the store this afternoon?

Ann: (No, I will. / I'm sorry, but I can't.)

B   주어진 명령문을 1번처럼 정중하게 요청하는 표현으로 바꾸어 쓰시오.

1   Buy some milk for me.

   Can you please buy some milk for me   ?

2   Call me back later.

Could ______________________________ ?

3   Send an e-mail to Jane.

Will ______________________________ ?

4   Turn on the lights.

Can ______________________________ ?

5   File these reports.

Would ______________________________ ?

6   Answer the phone.

Could ______________________________ ?

필요·의무를 나타내는 have to, must

Form

주어	have[has] to	동사원형
I/We/You/They	**have to**	**work** hard.
He/She	**has to**	

주어		must	동사원형
I/You/He/She/We/They		**must**	**work** hard.

Do/Does	주어	have to	동사원형	긍정 응답			부정 응답		
Do	I	**have to**	**work** hard?	Yes,	you	**do.**	No,	you	**don't.**
Does	he				he	**does.**		he	**doesn't.**

Meaning & Use

1_ have to와 must는 필요나 의무를 나타낸다. have to가 대개 다른 이에 의해 주어지는 의무를 나타내는 데 반해, must는 자신이 느끼는 필요나 법에 의해 주어지는 의무를 나타낸다.

I have to do the job for Mike.

Drivers must obey all traffic lights.

2_ must는 과거와 미래형이 없어서 have to의 과거형과 미래형을 대신 사용한다. 과거는 had to, 미래는 will have to로 쓴다.

We had to finish our homework by 6:00 yesterday evening.

I'll have to finish writing the report by tomorrow.

3_ have to와 must의 현재형은 현재뿐 아니라 미래의 필요나 의무도 나타낼 수 있다.

I have to work now/tomorrow/next weekend.

I must do some shopping now/tonight/next week.

4_ have to의 의문문은 일반동사처럼 do동사를 사용한다.

"Do you have to work late every day?" "Yes, I do."

"Did you have to take the exam yesterday?" "No, I didn't."

A have to, has to를 사용하여 문장을 완성하시오.

1 A cook _______________ keep his or her hands clean.

2 An army officer _______________ wear a uniform.

3 Doctors _______________ be careful about treating patients.

4 A porter _______________ carry people's baggage.

5 Secretaries _______________ be good at typing.

B 1번처럼 have to, has to를 사용하여 대화를 완성 하시오.

1 A: Is Jason getting up early this morning?
   B: Yes, *he has to get up early this morning*. He has a math test today.

2 A: Is Beth leaving early today?
   B: Yes, _______________________. She has an appointment with her doctor.

3 A: Are you going shopping this afternoon?
   B: Yes, _______________________________. There's no food at home.

4 A: Are you and your wife taking a taxi to school?
   B: Yes, _______________________________. Our car isn't working.

5 A: Is your father working late today?
   B: Yes, _______________________________. He has a lot of things to do.

C have/has to, had to를 사용하여 다음 문장을 완성하시오.

1 Mary _______________ take an entrance exam last year.

2 Judy has an appointment with her dentist. She _______________ leave early tomorrow.

3 I _______________ go to New York for a meeting tomorrow.

4 My sister _______________ work on Saturdays.

5 You _______________ drive on the left in England.

Form

주어	do/does not	have to	동사원형
I/We/You/They	**do not**	**have to**	**stop** here.
He/She	**does not**		

주어	must not	동사원형
I/You/He/She/We/They	**must not**	**stop** here.
	mustn't	

Meaning & Use

1_ have to와 must의 부정은 그 뜻이 서로 다르다. have to의 부정인 don't have to는 "~할 필요가 없다"는 뜻의 불필요를 나타낸다.

Tomorrow is Sunday. You don't have to get up early.

You don't have to go to school by bus. I'll drive you to school.

2_ must의 부정인 must not은 "~해서는 안 된다"는 뜻의 강한 금지를 나타내며 mustn't로 축약하여 쓸 수 있다.

You mustn't smoke here.

In soccer, you mustn't touch the ball with your hands.

3_ don't have to의 과거형은 didn't have to이나 must not의 과거형은 없다.

We didn't have to wait very long for the bus.

I didn't have to go to work yesterday.

Key point_ don't have to와 need not

학교 내신시험에서는 이 단원에서 공부한 don't have to와 must not의 차이를 종종 출제한다. 이와 관련하여 don't have to를 need not으로 바꾸어 나타낼 수 있음도 꼭 기억해야 한다.

You don't have to work today.

= You need not work today.

A must와 mustn't를 써서 문장을 완성하시오.

1 You ___________ make a noise in the classroom.

2 You ___________ stop at the stop sign.

3 You ___________ drive without a driver's license.

4 You ___________ use a cell phone on a plane.

5 You ___________ speak politely on the phone.

6 You ___________ play with a knife.

7 You ___________ arrive in class on time.

B mustn't와 don't/doesn't have to를 써서 문장을 완성하시오.

1 You _____________ close the windows. I'll close them later.

2 Eric _____________ call Jane. She knows about it already.

3 We _____________ take food into the library.

4 She isn't working tomorrow, so she _____________ get up early.

5 You _____________ call people after 9:00 in the evening.

6 You _____________ buy tickets at the box office. You can buy them online.

7 We _____________ pay in cash. We can use a credit card.

C 문맥에 맞게 mustn't와 don't/doesn't have to를 써 넣으시오.

1 There isn't much time left, so we _____________ waste it.

2 We _____________ hurry. We have enough time.

3 You _____________ stay up late. You have to get up at 6:00.

4 You _____________ stay up late to finish the work. You can do it tomorrow.

5 We _____________ leave the door open. Thieves will break in.

6 We _____________ leave the door open. I have the key.

7 You _____________ call Sue about this. She already knows about it.

8 You _____________ call Sue about this. Let's keep it a secret.

충고를 나타내는 should, had better

Form

주어	조동사 (not)	동사원형	
I/You/He/She/We/They	should (not) had better (not) 'd better (not)	forget	about it.

Meaning & Use

1 _ 상대방에게 "~하는 것이 좋겠다"고 충고나 조언을 할 때 should를 쓴다.

You should be careful about taking the exam.

You should do your best.

2 _ had better도 충고나 조언할 때 쓰며, 일상 영어에서는 'd better로 축약하여 쓴다.

It's raining. You'd better take an umbrella with you.

We'd better not be late or we'll miss the plane.

3 _ should와 had better의 부정은 뒤에 not을 두어 should not, had better not으로 쓴다.
should not은 축약하여 shouldn't로 쓸 수 있다.

You shouldn't stay up late. You have a math exam tomorrow.

You'd better not do it again.

4 _ must는 반드시 해야 하는 필요나 의무를 말할 때 쓰고, should는 어느 것이 좋은 지에 대해서
충고할 때 쓴다.

You must stop smoking, or you'll die.

You really should stop smoking. It's bad for you.

A   should와 shouldn't를 사용하여 문장을 완성하시오.

1   You ___________ be unkind to foreigners.

2   We ___________ eat a lot of fruit and vegetables.

3   You ___________ drive for many hours without stopping.

4   In a big city, you ___________ be careful about walking down the street.

5   You ___________ drink too much coffee, or you can't sleep.

6   He watches TV all the time. He ___________ watch TV that much.

7   It's late and you're tired. You ___________ go to bed now.

B   'd better와 주어진 어구를 사용하여 문장을 완성하시오.

look for	not sit	not drink	call	take	go	not start

1   This milk smells funny. We ___________________ it.

2   Eric doesn't like his job. He ___________________ a new job.

3   The chair looks very dirty. You ___________________ on it.

4   The baby's temperature is 40℃. We ___________________ the doctor.

5   I have a toothache. I ___________________ to the dentist.

6   You ___________________ smoking, or you won't be able to stop.

7   I have an important interview. I ___________________ a taxi.

C   must와 should를 문맥에 맞게 써 넣으시오.

1   "Do I look all right?" "You ___________ get a haircut."

2   According to the law, everyone ___________ respect the rights of others.

3   You look tired. You ___________ get some rest.

4   You ___________ be over 18 to get married.

5   Erica really cares about you. You ___________ follow her advice.

6   You know, I think you ___________ take a vacation.

7   The law says that drivers ___________ take another road.

Form

	주어	조동사	동사원형	
	You/He/She/They	must	be	sick.
		can't		
		may		
		might		

Meaning & Use

1 _ 어떤 일이 사실이라는 확신이 있을 때는 must를 쓰며 "~임에 틀림없다"는 뜻을 나타낸다. 이 의미로는 have to를 쓰지 않는다.

There's someone at the door. It must be the mailman.

Hello. Nice to meet you. You must be Lucy's husband.

2 _ 어떤 일이 사실이 아니라고 확신을 갖는 경우 can't를 쓰며 "~일 리가 없다"는 뜻을 나타낸다.

You had lunch one hour ago. You can't be hungry.

I saw Amy at the library a minute ago, so she can't be at home.

3 _ 어떤 일이 일어날 가능성에 대해 확신이 없을 때는 may나 might를 쓰며 "~일지도 모른다" 는 뜻을 나타낸다.

"Is Jack from Canada?" "He may/might be, I'm not sure."

Lisa may/might not come to school tomorrow. She's a little sick today.

Key point _ **may be vs. maybe**

학교 내신시험에서는 may be와 maybe를 구별할 것을 요구하는 문제를 가끔 출제한다. may be가 "조동사+동사원형"임에 반해, maybe는 "아마도"라는 뜻의 부사임을 명심하자.

She may be right. (O) / She maybe right. (X)

Maybe she is right. (O) / May be she is right. (X)

A 주어진 사실과 이에 적절히 연결될 추측을 골라 밑줄에 그 기호를 쓰시오.

_____ 1 The woman's name is Michelle. a. She might be sick.

_____ 2 He's only fourteen. b. He must be older than twenty.

_____ 3 She looks pale. c. She may be French.

_____ 4 She's wearing a wedding ring. d. They may not be at home.

_____ 5 The house is dark. e. She may be very rich.

_____ 6 He has gray hair. f. She must be married.

_____ 7 She showed me a lot of money. g. He can't be married.

B must와 can't를 써서 문장을 완성하시오.

1 A is bigger than B, and B is bigger than C, then A ___________ be bigger than C.

2 Jane ___________ have a problem. She keeps crying.

3 The doorbell is ringing. It ___________ be Jenny."

"No, it ___________ be Jenny. It's too early."

4 You had lunch half an hour ago. You ___________ be hungry.

5 Diana ___________ know Tokyo very well. She lived there for five years.

6 Erica lives in a very small apartment. She ___________ be rich.

7 She always tries to help the poor. She ___________ be a good person.

C may/might, must, can't를 써서 문장을 완성하시오.

1 "What's that animal?" "I'm not sure. It ___________ be a rabbit."

2 They have two houses and two big cars. They ___________ be rich.

3 Mark studied very hard, but he got poor grades. He _________ be very smart.

4 "What are your plans for next year?" "I'm not sure. I ___________ go to Canada."

5 "There's someone at the door. I think it's Bill."

"It ___________ be Bill. He's in Australia now."

6 "There's someone at the door." "It ___________ be Jim. He always comes home at this time of the day."

A   잘못된 부분을 바르게 고치시오.

1   They could saw something in the dark.

2   I cann't leave right now.

3   Judy should buys some sugar to make a cake.

4   Should he meets his manager tomorrow?

5   Ann cans sing and dance very well.

6   I missed the first train. What I should do?

7   "May I smoke here?" "No, you mayn't."

8   Would please you help me?

9   We have leave tonight.

10   Tom must finishes the work by 6:00.

11   Didn't you see the sign? You don't have to smoke here.

12   Fred will able to drive by the end of this month.

13   We will can get to the meeting on time.

14   She will must take the test next week.

15   I can't went to the party last week.

16   You better wear a sweater. It's going to get cold.

17   You don't have wash the dishes. I'll do it later.

18   Alice was able fix the radio by herself yesterday.

19   You'd not better be late for the seminar.

20   Diana must to work late last week to finish the project.

21   You must to drive on the right in this country.

22   Does she has to leave right now?

23   They maybe right.

24   You don't had better quit the job.

25   She couldn't able to save her son.

B 다음 밑줄 친 부분에 가장 적절한 것을 고르시오.

1 A: Can they play the guitar?
B: No, _____________.
a. they can   b. they could
c. they can't   d. they couldn't

2. A few years ago, they _____________ build a bridge.
a. can   b. couldn't
c. can't   d. cannot

3. You _____________ take the bus to work. I'll drive you there.
a. must   b. don't have to
c. should   d. have to

4. You _______ sit there. Just make yourself at home.
a. mustn't   b. can't
c. had to   d. can

5. Be careful with that glass. You _____________ it.
a. might breaks   b. break
c. may not break   d. might break

6. A: I'm cold.
B: _____________ put on a coat.
a. You better   b. You'd better
c. You'd should   d. You might

7. You _____________ do it now. I'll do it later.
a. doesn't have to   b. don't has to
c. don't have to   d. have to

8. _____________ smoke anywhere in school.
a. You can   b. You may
c. You can't   d. You don't have to

9. _____________ your cell phone?
a. May I use   b. May use
c. I may use   d. I may not use

10. A: I can't speak English, but I'm moving to Canada soon.
B: You _____________ English classes.
a. should take   b. have take
c. shouldn't   d. may take

11. A: Is Ann going to buy a TV?
    B: No, she ___________ buy one. Her mother gave her a TV set.
    a. don't have to
    b. doesn't has to
    c. has to
    d. doesn't have to

12. A: May I stay out until midnight?
    B: No, you ___________ .
    a. may
    b. can
    c. might not
    d. may not

13. A: Would you close the door, please?   B: ___________
    a. Certainly.
    b. Yes, I could.
    c. Yes, I would.
    d. No, I can't.

14. Jim can't speak French now, but after a few lessons he ________ speak
    a little.
    a. can't
    b. was able to
    c. could
    d. will be able to

15. You ________ hand in your homework on time, or you'll get poor grades.
    a. better not
    b. 'd better not
    c. 'd better
    d. 'd not better

16. A: Could you please explain that again?   B: Yes, ___________
    a. I could.
    b. not at all.
    c. I do.
    d. of course.

17. ___________ I borrow your pen, please?
    a. May
    b. Would
    c. Should
    d. Will

18. I ___________ go to the supermarket. I need some sugar for this cake.
    a. might
    b. must
    c. could
    d. may

19. We ___________ leave now. It's getting late.
    a. could
    b. should
    c. might
    d. would

20. Last week, I ___________ get a ticket to the concert.
    a. can
    b. was able to
    c. am able to
    d. were able to

21. A: What should we have for lunch?
    B: ___________ pizza.
    a. We have to have   b. We'd better have
    c. We must have   d. We're able to have

22. ___________ you carry these boxes for me, please?
    a. May   b. Could
    c. Should   d. Might

23. The road is dangerous. You ___________ be careful.
    a. had better not   b. mustn't
    c. could   d. had better

24. You ___________ drink and drive.
    a. should   b. had better
    c. mustn't   d. have to

25. Joe went to bed at 2:00 and got up at 5:00. He ___________ be very tired.
    a. doesn't have to   b. can't
    c. must   d. should

26. She isn't working tomorrow, so she ___________ get up early.
    a. don't have to   b. doesn't have to
    c. mustn't   d. shouldn't

27. What was wrong with you? Why ___________ go to the hospital?
    a. had you do   b. did you have to
    c. mustn't you   d. shouldn't you

28. You just had lunch. You ___________ be hungry yet.
    a. mustn't   b. shouldn't
    c. can't   d. may not

29. You worked ten hours today. You ___________ be really tired.
    a. must   b. can
    c. may   d. might

30. What time ___________ go to the dentist tomorrow?
    a. you must   b. you have to
    c. have you to   d. do you have to

Chapter 11

수동태

Form

주 어	be + 과거분사		by + 목적어
Dinner	**is**	**cooked**	**by** Susie.
	was		

Meaning & Use

1_ 주어가 동작을 행하여 '~하다' 의 의미를 나타내는 문장 형식을 능동태라고 하고, 주어가 동작의 대상이 되어 '~되다, 당하다' 의 의미를 나타내는 형식을 수동태라고 한다.

My mom loves me.　　　(능동태)

→ I am loved by my mom. (수동태)

2_ 수동태를 만드는 방법은 다음과 같다.

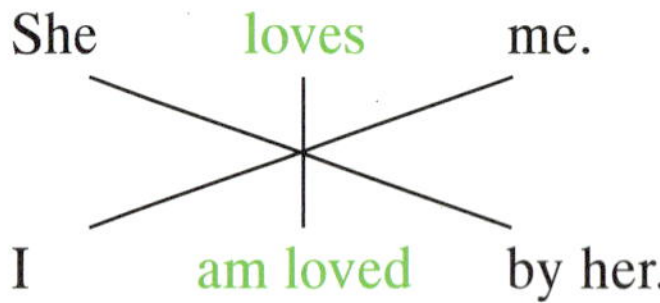

■ 능동태의 목적어는 수동태의 주어가 된다. (me → I)

■ 능동태의 동사를 「be동사+과거분사」의 형태로 바꾸어 수동태의 동사로 한다.
be 동사는 주어의 인칭과 수에 일치시키고, 시제는 능동태의 시제와 일치시킨다.
(loves → am loved)

■ 능동태의 주어는 「by+목적격」으로 바꾸어 문장 끝에 둔다. (She → by her)

3_ 과거분사는 규칙동사의 경우 동사에 -ed를 붙이면 되므로 과거와 형태가 같다.

play – played – played　　　love – loved – loved

study – studied – studied　　stop – stopped – stopped

4_ 일부 동사의 과거분사는 불규칙하게 변한다.

cut – cut – cut　　　buy – bought – bought

drink – drank – drunk　　give – gave – given

A 다음 중 적절한 것을 고르시오.

1   This window (broke / was broken) by your little boy.

2   This book (wrote / was written) by my father.

3   The new university (will open / will be opened) by the President.

4   Tim (was driving / was driven) too fast, and he (stopped / was stopped) by the police.

5   The child (found / was found) by a neighbor last night.

6   All the work (will do / will be done) by machines in the future.

7   Helen (invites / is invited) us every weekend.

B 다음 문장을 수동태로 고치시오.

1   The teacher loves us.

____

2   Sue checks the letters every day.

____

3   He invites her to the party.

____

4   Mary keeps the files in the cabinet.

____

5   Susie wrote the report.

____

6   Ted sold the car.

____

7   We sent e-mails to them.

____

8   I saw Nancy at the concert.

____

Form

주어	be + 과거분사		by + 목적어
	is		
The report	**was**	**examined**	**by** Julie.
	will be		

주어	조동사 + be + 과거분사		by + 목적어
	can		
The report	**should**	**be examined**	**by** Julie.
	has to		

Meaning & Use

1_ 수동태의 시제는 be 동사의 시제로 나타낸다. 현재시제는 「be 동사 현재형 (am/is/are)+과거분사」로, 과거시제는 「be 동사 과거형 (was/were)+과거분사」로 그리고 미래시제는 「be 동사 미래형 (will be)+과거분사」로 나타낸다.

Books change your life.

→ Your life is changed by books.

Books changed your life.

→ Your life was changed by books.

Books will change your life.

→ Your life will be changed by books.

2_ 조동사가 있는 문장의 수동태는 「조동사+be 동사+과거분사」형태가 된다.

Ann must finish the work.

→ The work must be finished by Ann.

Ann can finish the work.

→ The work can be finished by Ann.

Ann should finish the work.

→ The work should be finished by Ann.

A 다음 문장을 수동태로 바꾸어 쓰시오.

1 Fred takes a test every week.

____

2 Edison invented the phonograph.

____

3 The manager will check the data.

____

4 Jason loves Juliet.

____

5 I will finish the homework soon.

____

6 The dog bit him yesterday.

____

B 다음 문장을 수동태로 바꾸어 쓰시오.

1 I'm going to give a present to Mary.

____

2 Mr. Kim may teach us.

____

3 Frank should write a letter to the customers.

____

4 You must finish this work by 5:00.

____

5 I have to do the work now.

____

6 Joe can draw beautiful pictures.

____

7 Mary might solve the problem.

____

Form

주어	be not + 과거분사		by + 목적어
The report	**is not**	examined	**by** Julie.
	was not		

Be	주어	과거분사	by + 목적어
Is	the report	examined	**by** Julie?
Was			

Meaning & Use

1 _   수동태의 부정은 be 동사 뒤에 not을 두어 「be 동사+not+과거분사」형식이 된다.

George didn't send an e-mail to me.

→ An e-mail was not sent to me by George.

2 _   의문문의 수동태는 「Be 동사+주어+과거분사 ~?」형식이 된다.

Did you clean the room?

→ Was the room cleaned by you?

3 _   의문문의 수동태는 어려워 보이지만 다음과 같은 과정을 따르면 쉽게 이해할 수 있다.

Did you finish the work?

→ You finished the work. (평서문으로)

→ The work was finished by you. (평서문을 수동태로)

→ Was the work finished by you? (수동태를 의문문으로)

Exercises

A 다음 문장을 수동태로 바꾸어 쓰시오.

1 Bob doesn't love Susie.

2 I didn't make this table.

3 Sue doesn't invite many friends to the party.

4 They didn't see Tom at the library.

5 The company doesn't send e-mails to the customers.

6 Sophia didn't find the file.

B 다음 문장을 수동태로 바꾸어 쓰시오.

1 Did Ted meet Sue?

2 Does Mr. Smith teach science?

3 Did the students take a math exam?

4 Do you clean the computer room?

5 Did Ann invite you to the dinner?

6 Does Fred check the report?

7 Did Joe send the mail to the customer?

Form

주어	be + 과거분사		(by + 목적어)
English	**is spoken**	in Canada.	
My car	**was repaired**	yesterday.	

주어	be + 과거분사	by 외의 전치사 + 목적어
The students	**are interested**	in computer games.
The mountains	**were covered**	with snow.

Meaning & Use

1_ 수동태에서 행위자는 「by+목적어」로 나타낸다. 그러나 행위자가 막연한 일반 사람을 나타내는 by us, by them, by people이거나, 행위자가 누구인지 불명확한 by someone인 경우에는 「by+목적어」를 생략할 수 있다.

English is spoken in America (by people).

That building was built ten years ago (by someone).

2_ 일반적으로 수동태에서는 행위자를 「by+목적어」로 나타내지만 by 이외의 전치사를 쓰는 수동태가 있으므로 주의하여야 한다.

The news surprised us.

→ We were surprised at/by the news.

The snow covers the mountains.

→ The mountains are covered with snow.

I'm interested in his idea.

The desk is made of wood.

We're worried about your health.

The box is filled with apples.

Lisa was pleased with the Christmas present.

Exercises

A   다음 중 적절한 것을 고르시오.

1   English (speaks / is spoken) in Australia.

2   Money (borrow / is borrowed) at the bank.

3   The BMW (makes / is made) in Germany.

4   Diamonds (find / are found) in Australia.

5   Our windows (clean / are cleaned) once a month.

6   Mary (spends / is spent) too much money on clothes.

B   다음 문장을 수동태로 바꾸고, 가능한 경우 「by+목적어」를 생략하시오.

1   They pay me on the first day of every month.

____

2   They sent Julie to the Singapore office.

____

3   People eat a lot of chocolate in the United States.

____

4   Bell invented the telephone.

____

5   Someone built the tower in 1999.

____

C   다음 중 적절한 것을 고르시오.

1   She is interested (by / in) horse riding.

2   Our fingerprints were taken (by / with) the police.

3   The table is made (by / of) wood.

4   The road is covered (by / with) the leaves.

5   The basket is filled (by / with) the toys.

6   The table was made (by / of) Andrew.

A 잘못된 부분을 바르게 고치시오.

1. This picture was taken at my friend.

2. A lot of music programs is shown on TV on weekends.

3. E-mails are sent to the customers by she.

4. The children were took to the museum by the teacher.

5. The child is found by the police yesterday.

6. The washing machine is fixed by the repairman tomorrow.

7. The work will be finish by Jane.

8. The house will painted this week.

9. Concert tickets can buy at the box office.

10. English spoken all over the world.

11. Many languages can are heard in Hong Kong.

12. This table is made by wood.

13. I'm interested by modern jazz.

14. The secret has to keep between you and me.

15. The data should be check every three hours.

16. The letter has to sent by 5:00 this afternoon.

17. Was the Eiffel Tower build by Gustave Eiffel?

18. Alfred won't invited to the party.

19. The bell will be rang five times.

20. A tower is going to build on the top of the mountain.

21. The wallet was not find anywhere.

22. The house must be rebuilt a few years ago.

23. Does the computer have to repaired now?

24. The report is going to sent to the teacher today.

25. Will a new bridge build soon, or will the old bridge be repaired?

B 주어진 단어의 적절한 형태를 써서 수동태 문장으로 만드시오.

1 *Guernica* ______________ by Picasso. (paint)

2 The 1988 Olympic Games ______________ in Seoul. (hold)

3 Film ______________ in supermarkets. (sell)

4 Your math class ______________ by Mr. Park next Tuesday. (teach)

5 Two people ______________ in a car accident yesterday. (kill)

6 Most people ______________ at the end of the month. (pay)

7 Rice ______________ all over Asia. (grow)

8 Next week our office ______________ to Seoul. (move)

C 다음 단어를 사용하여 주어진 주어로 시작하는 문장을 만드시오.

1 Thomas Edison / the light bulb / invent

→ Thomas Edison ____.

→ The light bulb ____.

2 a cake / Susie / make / yesterday

→ Susie ____.

→ A cake ____.

3 all the students / the art museum / visit / every month

→ All the students ____.

→ The art museum ____.

4 the thief / the police / arrest / soon / will

→ The police ____.

→ The thief ____.

5 will / they / help us / next Saturday.

→ They ____.

→ We ____.

6 people / a lot of books / publish / every year

→ People ____.

→ A lot of books ____.

D 다음 밑줄 친 부분에 가장 적절한 것을 고르시오.

1 The story was written __________ Andrew Smith.
a. in
b. at
c. by
d. during

2 This newspaper __________ by many people.
a. reads
b. are read
c. is reading
d. is read

3 __________ these cars made in Germany?
a. Do
b. Was
c. Have
d. Are

4 A: When __________ the museum built?   B: In 1920. It's very old.
a. does
b. was
c. is
d. has

5 A lot of people __________ the movie.
a. saw
b. will be seen
c. were seen
d. must be seen

6 The data __________ soon.
a. will check
b. is checked
c. will be checked
d. checks

7 A: When can you finish the work?
B: It __________ by this weekend.
a. might finish
b. may finish
c. might be finished
d. must finish

8 The hospital __________ next year.
a. is closed
b. is closes
c. was closed
d. will be closed

9 We __________ to the party last week.
a. didn't invite
b. weren't invited
c. didn't invited
d. wasn't invited

10 A: Where __________ born?   B: In Seattle.
a. were you
b. you were
c. was you
b. are you

11 I took the bus this morning because my car __________.

    a. is broken   b. was broken

    c. break   d. breaks

12 Chinese __________ in Hong Kong.

    a. speaks   b. spoken

    c. is spoken   d. are spoken

13 Stamps __________ at this store.

    a. isn't sold   b. sell

    c. aren't sold   d. sold

14 Some day English __________ everywhere.

    a. speaks   b. was spoken

    c. will be spoken   d. is spoken

15 Yesterday, e-mails __________ to all the members of the club.

    a. is sent   b. was sent

    c. were sent   d. are sent

16 This machine __________ tomorrow.

    a. is going to fix   b. is going to fixed

    c. is going to be fixed   d. is going be fixed

17 A: Look at this beautiful picture.

    B: __________ by you?

    a. Were it taken   b. Was it taken

    c. Was taken it   d. Were taken it

18 J. K. Rowling __________ the Harry Potter series.

    a. wrote   b. was written

    c. is written   d. is writing

19 English __________ in Canada.

    a. spoke   b. speak

    c. is spoken   d. speaks

20 The students __________ English for three years in middle school.

    a. teach   b. is taught

    c. was taught   d. were taught

Chapter 12

시제 종합 정리

Form

> **1** What **does** she **do** for a living?
> What **is** she **doing** right now?
>
> **2** Water **boils** at 100℃.
> Susan **plays** table tennis every Sunday.
>
> **3** Thomas Edison **invented** the phonograph.
> Orin **was taking** a shower at 7:00 yesterday evening.
> Michelle **was drawing** a picture when her mother **got** home from work.

Meaning & Use

1 _ 단순시제란 현재시제, 과거시제, 미래시제를 가리킨다. 반면 진행형이란 현재진행형, 과거진행형, 미래진행형을 말한다. 단순시제와 진행형의 가장 중요한 차이는 단순시제가 전반적인 때에 관한 사항을 말하는 데 반해, 진행형은 일정한 한 시점에서만 일어나는 사항을 나타낸다는 것이다.

2 _ 현재시제는 현재의 전반적인 상황을 나타낸다. 반면 현재진행형은 "바로 지금" 일어나고 있는 일만을 설명한다.

We study music every day.

We are studying music right now.

3 _ 현재시제는 현재의 전반적인 상황뿐만 아니라 변하지 않는 진리나 반복적인 습관 등도 나타낸다. 이것은 현재시제의 쓰임새가 보다 확대된 것으로 이해될 수 있다.

Light travels faster than sound.

4 _ 과거시제는 본래 과거에 일어났던 일을 나타내는데, 이 쓰임새가 확대되어 역사적 사실도 과거시제로 표현될 수 있다. 반면 과거진행형은 과거의 어느 한 시점에 일어나고 있었던 일을 가리킨다. 또한, 과거에 하나의 동작이 계속되고 있는데 다른 동작이 이를 방해하는 경우에 방해하는 동작은 과거시제로, 방해 받는 동작은 과거진행형으로 나타낸다.

It was snowing hard when I got up.

A   적절한 것을 괄호 안에서 고르시오.

1   Andy (plays, is playing) tennis every Saturday.

2   Right now, we (learn, are learning) how to make chicken soup.

3   Judy always (is laughing, laughs) at my jokes.

4   We learned that the earth (is moving, moves) around the sun.

5   We (watch, are watching) *Buffy the Vampire Slayer* every Thursday.

6   Ms. Baker (now talks, is now talking) to her friend on the phone.

7   We (usually have, are usually having) breakfast together.

B   주어진 동사의 과거시제나 과거진행형 중에서 적절한 것으로 문장을 완성하시오.

1   The phone (ring) ___________ when he was taking a shower.

2   Anthony (read) ___________ a newspaper when he heard a strange noise.

3   John came to visit Marie when she (do) ___________ her homework.

4   They (build) ___________ the bridge last year.

5   We (play) ___________ soccer at 3:00 yesterday afternoon.

6   Alexander Graham Bell (invent) ___________ the telephone.

7   I (take) ___________ a shower at 7:00 yesterday evening.

C   주어진 동사의 과거시제나 과거진행형 중에서 적절한 것으로 문장을 완성하시오.

1   Christopher Columbus (discover) ___________ America in 1492.

2   We (watch) ___________ our favorite show when someone knocked
     at the door.

3   What (do) ___________ you ___________ at this time yesterday?

4   Unfortunately, I (lose) ___________ my wallet on the subway.

5   A terrible accident (happen) ___________ when we were taking a walk.

6   I (visit) ___________ Italy in 1997.

7   Marie Curie (discover) ___________ radium in 1898.

Form

> **1** We **live** in Los Angeles.
>   We **have lived** in Los Angeles for two years.
>
> **2** We **have lived** in New York since 1988.
>   She **hasn't seen** him for many years.
>   **Has** she **finished** her homework yet?
>
> **3** She**'s been** to Paris several times.
>   She **went** to Paris last year.

Meaning & Use

1_ 완료형이란 두 시제를 연결하여 나타내는 표현 방식으로 현재완료형이 대표적이다.
「have/has+과거분사」의 형식으로 과거에 시작된 일이 현재에도 영향을 끼침을 표현한다. 단
순현재형이 현재라는 한 때를 나타내는 데 반해, 현재완료는 과거와 현재 모두와 연결된다는
점이 다르다.

He works for the company. (only the present)

He has worked for the company since 2000. (both the past and the present)

2_ 현재완료형의 평서문은 「주어+have/has+과거분사 ~」로, 부정문은 「주어+have/has+not+과
거분사 ~」로, 의문문은 「Have/Has+주어+과거분사 ~?」로 구성한다.

She has never been to Canada.

Have they finished their work yet?

3_ 앞서 살펴본 것처럼 현재완료형은 과거와 현재를 연결하기 때문에 yesterday, last year, in
2000와 같이 과거만을 나타내는 표현과는 함께 쓸 수 없다. 대신 since (~이래로 계속), for (~
동안), How long ~?(얼마나 오래 ~?)와 같이 과거와 현재를 연결하는 표현과 어울릴 수 있다.

I have known Buffy for over ten years.

I have met Buffy yesterday. (X)

I met Buffy yesterday. (O)

A 과거와 현재완료 동사형 중에서 적절한 것을 고르시오.

1 I (read / have read) the book since last week.

2 I (read / have read) the book last week.

3 My friend is a writer. He (wrote / has written) many books since 1998.

4 Shakespeare (wrote / has written) many plays.

5 I (didn't play / have never played) rugby last week.

6 My daughter (didn't speak / has never spoken) to me since she moved out.

7 (Did you met / Have you met) Dan before?

8 (Did you meet / Have you met) Dan yesterday?

B 밑줄 친 부분이 어법에 맞으면 C, 맞지 않으면 I 라고 쓰고 맞게 고치시오.

1 <u>Have you heard</u> the news on the radio last night? ( ) ________________

2 Susan isn't here. She<u>'s gone</u> to Hong Kong.   ( ) ________________

3 Where <u>have you been</u> last night?   ( ) ________________

4 Where <u>have you been</u> this week?   ( ) ________________

5 What time <u>have you finished</u> work yesterday?   ( ) ________________

6 I <u>have graduated</u> from middle school in 2003.   ( ) ________________

7 I'm leaving. I<u>'ve finished</u> my work.   ( ) ________________

C 주어진 동사의 과거나 현재완료형으로 문장을 완성하시오.

1 I ________________ (finish) my work at four o'clock.

2 I ________________ to New York many times. (be)

3 I ________________ to my parents yesterday. (write)

4 Somebody ________________ my umbrella last night. (take)

5 We ________________ too much yesterday. (eat)

6 Julie ________________ in a restaurant for two years (work). And then she left.

7 Who ________________ me last night? (call)

Form

주어	have / has	already / just	과거분사	yet
I	**have**	**just**	**finished**	my homework.
Susie	**has**	**already**	**seen**	the show.
He	**hasn't**		**arrived**	**yet.**

Meaning & Use

1_ 현재완료는 과거에 시작한 일이 현재에 끝났음을 나타내며, just, already, yet 등의 부사와 쓰인다.

The plane has just arrived. / I've already read the newspaper.

Jim hasn't left yet.

2_ already는 '이미, 벌써'의 뜻으로 긍정문이나 의문문에 쓰이며 have와 과거분사 사이 또는 문장 끝에 놓인다.

I've already met Karl. / You're late. We've started already.

3_ yet은 부정문과 의문문에 쓰인다. 부정문에 쓰이면 '아직'의 뜻이며, 의문문에 쓰이면 '이미, 벌써'의 뜻이다. 주로 문장 끝에 쓰인다.

"Have you spoken to Jack yet?" "No, not yet. He hasn't come in yet."

4_ just는 '지금 막, 방금'의 뜻으로 have와 과거분사 사이에 온다.

I've just come back from Tokyo. / The rain has just stopped.

Key point _ just vs. just now

학교 내신시험에서는 just와 just now가 현재완료 또는 과거와 어울리는지를 측정하는 문제를 종종 출제한다. just가 "방금"의 뜻으로 현재완료와 함께 쓰일 수 있는 데 반해, just now 는 "방금 전에"라는 뜻으로 분명히 과거를 나타내기 때문에 현재완료와 어울릴 수 없음에 특히 유의하자.

I've just finished doing my homework. (O)

I've just now finished doing my homework. (X)

A 주어진 어구의 적절한 형태와 already를 써서 다음 대화를 완성하시오.

get up	go	leave	make	pay	meet

1 "What time are you going to meet Annie?" "I ___________________ her."

2 "Where's Peter?" "He ___________________ to the concert."

3 "Should I pay?" "No, I ________________."

4 "Can you wake Kate up?" "She ________________."

5 "Let's make chicken soup." "I ________________ sandwiches."

6 "When does the last bus leave?" "It ________________."

B already나 yet을 써서 문장을 완성하시오.

1 It isn't a good party. Most people have __________ gone home.

2 My brother has __________ sold his old car.

3 It's eleven o'clock, but you haven't finished the work __________.

4 Her English class hasn't started __________.

5 I've __________ mailed the invitations.

6 I haven't eaten anything __________.

C 주어진 어구와 just를 써서 다음 대화를 완성하시오.

1 A: Where's Judy?
   B: (She / leave) _She's just left_________ for the airport.

2 A: Are you hungry?
   B: No, (I / have) ___________________ lunch.

3 A: Please call Mary this afternoon.
   B: (I / call) ________________ her.

4 A: (We / come) ________________ from the party.
   B: Did you have a good time?

5 A: How's Andrew?
   B: He's very happy. (He / finish) ___________________ his exams.

6 A: (I / receive) ________________ a letter from Lora.
   B: Oh, really? What did she say?

A 잘못된 부분을 바르게 고치시오.

1   She has give a present to her friend.

2   Jack has took a test for two hours.

3   He has the car for three years.

4   He has gone to the U.S. three years ago.

5   When have you come here?

6   How long do you worked in the factory?

7   I worked here since 1990.

8   He has seen never a French movie.

9   I lived in Seoul since 2001.

10   Have you eaten ever crabs?

11   How long you've been a teacher?

12   I haven't eaten dinner already.

13   How often has you been to Hawaii?

14   How much coffee have you drunk last night?

15   "Did he gone to Paris?" "Yes, he went to Paris last week."

16   Have you ever study science?

17   Is she done the homework yet?

18   I know Cecil for half a year.

19   Where have you been? I haven't seen you since a long time.

20   He's lived in the house for a long time, and then he moved to a new house.

21   Have arrived Jane and her husband?

22   I have be to Singapore many times.

23   "What's the matter?" "I have lose my keys."

24   When have you lost your keys?

25   How many times did you visited the office?

B 주어진 단어를 써서 문장을 완성하시오.

> already   yet   just now

1 A: Have you finished your homework?

B: Yes, I've ___________ finished it.

2 A: Are you going to send an e-mail to Jane?

B: I've ___________ done it.

3 A: I haven't finished my homework ___________.

B: You'd better finish it soon.

4 A: When did you meet Sally?

B: I met her ___________.

5 A: Did you have a meal?

B: We had lunch ___________.

6 A: What are you going to do?

B: I don't know. I haven't decided ___________.

C 주어진 동사의 현재완료형으로 다음 대화를 완성하시오.

1 A: I ___________ (buy) tickets for the concert. Do you want to come with me?

B: Sorry, but I'm too busy with work.

2 A: Look! I ___________ (find) some money.

B: Wow, you're so lucky.

3 A: You look happy.

B: Yes, I ___________ (pass) the exam.

4 A: Where's Robert?

B: He ___________ (just go) out.

5 A: Do you like skiing?

B: I ___________ (never try) it.

6 A: What time does the seminar start?

B: It ___________ (already start)

D 다음 밑줄 친 부분에 가장 적절한 것을 고르시오.

1 __________ you ever played football, Ted?

   a. Did   b. Have

   c. Has   d. Was

2 Why __________ you go to the library after class?

   a. did   b. have

   c. were   d. are

3 Joe __________ in that company for five years.

   a. works   b. was

   c. is working   d. has worked

4 You're a computer programmer. How long __________ this work?

   a. did you done   b. do you do

   c. have you done   d. were you doing

5 I've been a police officer since __________.

   a. a long time   b. 2002

   c. two years   d. a few months

6 Karl __________ to Italy five times.

   a. was   b. is

   c. has been   d. has go

7 __________ the drama for about a year.

   a. I'm watch   b. I've watched

   c. watch   d. I've watching

8 John has already __________ this course.

   a. takes   b. took

   c. taken   d. taking

9 The reporter hasn't finished his work __________.

   a. already   b. yet

   c. now   d. just

10 How many cups of coffee __________ this morning?

   a. have you drunk   b. do you drink

   c. have you drank   d. were you drunk

11 Amy ___________ Hong Kong four years ago.

a. has left
b. was left
c. was leaving
d. left

12 Ann and Andrew ___________ at C & C Company since 2001.

a. are working
b. has worked
c. have worked
d. worked

13 I have ___________ seen the movie.

a. already
b. yet
c. still
d. ever

14 "Has the mail come yet?" "Yes, it ___________."

a. did
b. have
c. has
d. is

15 ___________ you written an e-mail to Joan?

a. Did
b. Do
c. Have
d. Was

16 The team has ___________ won the first prize.

a. just
b. yet
c. ever
d. still

17 I ___________ to buy the car yet.

a. haven't decided
b. have decided
c. decided
d. am not decided

18 "Has Judy called yet?" "Yes, she ___________."

a. does
b. hasn't
c. call
d. has

19 Chris ___________ from Sidney.

a. is just arrived
b. just arrive
c. has just arrived
d. arrived just

20 Jack ___________ the report one hour ago.

a. has finished
b. finished
c. didn't finished
d. has already finished

Chapter 13

부정사

Form

to부정사	동사	형용사
To cook	is	fun.

가주어	동사	형용사	to부정사
It	is	fun	**to cook.**

주어	동사	부정사
They	decided	**to leave.**

Meaning & Use

1_ 「to + 동사원형」을 to부정사라 하며 문장에서 명사, 형용사, 부사 역할을 할 수 있다.

2_ to부정사의 명사적 용법이란 to부정사가 명사처럼 문장의 주어, 목적어, 보어로 쓰이는 경우를 말한다.

3_ to부정사가 주어로 쓰이는 경우는 격식체이며 대개 to부정사를 문장 뒤에 두고 주어 자리에는 특별한 의미가 없는 it을 쓰는데, 이 it을 '가주어' 라 하고 원래 주어인 부정사를 '진주어' 라고 한다.

To cook is fun. → It is fun to cook.

To master English is difficult. → It is difficult to master English.

4_ 다음 동사들 뒤에 동사가 목적어로 올 경우에는 to부정사를 써야 한다.

decide	hope	plan	promise	want	would like

Everybody wants to succeed.

He decided to call Andy.

5_ to부정사는 문장의 보어로 쓰일 수 있다.

My favorite hobby is to play MapleStory.

A 밑줄 친 부분에 to가 필요하면 써 넣고, 필요 없으면 X표 하시오.

1 I don't want _______ study at the library.

2 Do you _______ play baseball?

3 It's not easy _______ learn foreign languages.

4 It may _______ snow this weekend.

5 Michelle planned _______ go on a diet.

6 I would like _______ talk with you for a minute.

B 주어진 동사의 원형 또는 to부정사를 사용하여 문장을 완성하시오.

come	buy	visit	see	repair	have

1 It's important ___________ good friends.

2 I'll ___________ it next week.

3 I'm planning ___________ New York next month.

4 Ted promised ___________ to the meeting.

5 I would like ___________ the movie with Susie.

6 I will ___________ your watch by Tuesday.

C 가주어 it을 사용하여 올바른 문장을 만드시오.

1 be / useful / learn / a foreign language
   It is useful to learn a foreign language.

2 be / important / tell the truth

   ____

3 be / fun / meet new people

   ____

4 be / hard / master breakdancing

   ____

5 be / interesting / travel to new countries

   ____

Form

	명사/대명사	to부정사
It's	**time**	**to go**.
I have some	**letters**	**to write**.
Do you have	**anything**	**to read**?

Meaning & Use

1_ to부정사는 형용사처럼 명사나 대명사를 수식할 수 있다. 그러나 일반 형용사와는 달리 to부정사는 항상 명사나 대명사 뒤에서 수식하며 '~할'의 의미를 나타낸다.

I have some books to read.

I have a lot of things to do.

2_ 다음과 같은 명사 뒤에 흔히 to부정사가 쓰인다.

time	way	chance

It's time to go home.

I'll show you the way to use the copier.

I was waiting for a chance to talk to her.

3_ -thing, -body/one 뒤에 to부정사를 쓸 수 있다.

Do you have anything to read?

Have you found anybody to help you?

Key point_ **to**부정사와 전치사

학교 내신시험에서는 형용사적 용법의 to부정사에서 내용상 필요한 경우 전치사를 생략할 수 없다는 점을 종종 출제한다. to부정사의 꾸밈을 받는 명사를 to부정사 뒤로 위치시켜 보면 전치사가 필요한지 그렇지 않은지를 알 수 있다.

I have a pencil to write with. (O)   [~ to write with a pencil]

I have a pencil to write. (X)   [~ to write a pencil]

A 주어진 표현을 사용하여 문장을 완성하시오.

| homework to do | stories to tell | friend to meet |
| letters to send | money to lend | video to watch |

1 My father always has very interesting ____________ about his school life.

2 I can go to the concert because I have no ____________ tonight.

3 I'm going to the post office. Do you have any ____________?

4 I'll stay at home tonight. I have a good ____________.

5 I'll be home a little late tonight. I have a ____________ after work.

6 Sorry, I don't have any ____________ you.

B to부정사를 사용하여 문장을 완성하시오.

| learn | go | enter | take | see | win |

1 It's time ____________ a break.

2 There is no way ____________ the office.

3 She is waiting for a chance ____________ her children.

4 What's the best way ____________ English?

5 It's ____________ the game.

6 Buffy took the chance ____________ to the United States.

C to부정사를 사용하여 문장을 완성하시오.

| love | wear | carry | do | talk with | help |

1 I can't go to the party. I have nothing nice ____________.

2 There was nothing ____________. All the work was finished.

3 All my friends went to the concert, so I have no friends ____________.

4 Everybody needs someone ____________.

5 Have you found anybody ____________ you with the homework?

6 Your arms are full. Give me something ____________.

Form

1 We are **pleased to see** you.

2 He went to the United States **to study** English.

Meaning & Use

1_ to부정사의 부사적 용법은 크게 두 가지로 나뉜다. 첫 번째는 감정의 원인을 나타내는 경우이고, 두 번째는 행동의 구체적인 목적을 나타내는 경우이다.

2_ to부정사는 흔히 다음의 형용사 다음에 와서 형용사가 나타내는 감정의 원인을 설명한다.

glad	happy	pleased	sad	surprised

I'm pleased to meet you.

I was surprised to hear the news.

3_ to부정사는 일정한 행동의 구체적인 목적을 나타낼 수 있다.

Julie went to Paris to study music.

I turned on the TV to watch the news.

4_ 목적의 의미는 「for + 명사」로도 나타낼 수 있다.

He went to the store to buy some fruit.

He went to the store for some fruit.

Key point_ 감정의 원인 **vs.** 판단의 근거

학교 내신시험에서는 to부정사의 부사적 용법이 감정의 원인을 나타내는 경우와 일정한 판단의 근거를 나타내는 경우를 구별할 것을 종종 요구한다. to부정사 바로 앞에 오는 형용사를 보면 어느 경우인지 알 수 있는데, 판단의 근거인 경우에는 foolish, wise 등과 같은 형용사가 앞에 온다.

Erica was wise to listen to her heart. (판단의 근거)

Erica was sad to hear that her sister was so ill. (감정의 원인)

Exercises

A   주어진 표현을 사용하여 문장을 완성하시오.

> surprised to see glad to get sad to see
> pleased to eat happy to watch

1   We were _______________ them cry.

2   Was Julie _______________ you at the party?

3   I was _______________ your letter last week.

4   I was _______________ such delicious food.

5   I was _______________ a wonderful movie on the flight.

B   뜻이 통하는 문장이 되도록, 적절한 것을 골라 그 기호를 밑줄에 쓰시오.

_____ 1   I exercise every day   a. to buy a house.

_____ 2   I study hard   b. to text message my friends.

_____ 3   You must drive all night   c. to be healthy.

_____ 4   We must save a lot of money   d. to buy a sweater.

_____ 5   I'm going to the library   e. to pass the exam.

_____ 6   I bought a cell phone   f. to get to Chicago by tomorrow.

_____ 7   I went to the shopping mall   g. to study for the exam.

C   to 또는 for를 사용하여 문장을 완성하시오.

1   We went to the concert _______ see our favorite singers.

2   Sue wants to go to university _______ study music.

3   I went to the cafeteria _______ lunch.

4   I'm going to the supermarket _______ some milk and bread.

5   I drank a lot of coffee _______ stay awake.

6   We left early _______ get there on time.

7   We're going to Italy _______ a vacation.

Form

	too	형용사	to부정사	
		형용사	**to부정사**	
Sue is	**too**	**young**	**to go**	to school.
I am		**busy**	**to help**	you.

	형용사	enough	to부정사	
Andy is	**old**	**enough**	**to drive**	a car.
It is	**warm**		**to swim**	in the river.

	enough	명사	to부정사	
I have	**enough**	**money**	**to buy**	a house.
I have	**enough**	**eggs**	**to make**	an omelet.

Meaning & Use

1 _ too가 형용사와 함께 쓰이면 '필요 이상으로 지나치게' 라는 부정적인 의미를 나타내어, 「too + 형용사 + to부정사」는 '너무 ~하여 ~할 수 없다' 는 뜻이 된다.

I am too busy to help you.

I'm too tired to go out.

2 _ 「형용사 + enough + to부정사」는 '~할 만큼 충분히 ~한' 의 의미를 나타낸다. 중요한 것은 too가 형용사 앞에 오는데 비해 enough은 형용사 뒤에 온다는 점이다.

I'm old enough to drive a car.

Your English is good enough to talk with a native speaker.

3 _ enough이 명사와 함께 쓰일 경우에는 명사 앞에 놓여 「enough + 명사 + to부정사」의 형식이 된다.

He has enough money to buy a big car.

I have enough time to finish the work.

A   too 또는 enough을 넣어 문장을 완성하시오.

1   He was ____________ tired to get up early.

2   Do you have ___________ time to pick me up this morning?

3   Cindy isn't tall ___________ to ride the roller coaster.

4   The question was ___________ difficult to answer.

5   Do you have ___________ money to rent an apartment?

6   The piano is ___________ heavy to lift.

B   다음 두 문장을 too ~ to를 사용하여 한 문장으로 만드시오.

1   I was too short. I couldn't reach the ceiling.
    I was too short to reach the ceiling.

2   I am too weak. I can't carry the big bag.
    ____

3   We were too tired. We couldn't walk home.
    ____

4   I was too hungry. I couldn't do anything.
    ____

5   I felt too sad. I couldn't talk to anyone.
    ____

C   다음 두 문장을 enough to ~를 사용하여 한 문장으로 만드시오.

1   Jack can reach the ceiling. He is tall enough.
    Jack is tall enough to reach the ceiling.

2   Dan will pass the exam. He is smart enough.
    ____

3   Alex can play basketball. He is tall enough.
    ____

4   I can go on vacation. I have enough money.
    ____

5   Lucy couldn't pay the bill. She didn't have enough money.
    ____

A   잘못된 부분을 바르게 고치시오.

1   I decided buy a new car.

2   Is important to find a good job.

3   I went to the library for do my homework.

4   Do you want watch TV tonight?

5   I came here for see my sister.

6   I planned to visited Canada this summer.

7   Sometimes, it is important say no.

8   I would like see you again.

9   That is difficult to learn a foreign language.

10   Amy isn't enough old to get married.

11   Jack has money enough to buy a motorcycle.

12   I'm enough tired to walk home.

13   I'm glad see you here.

14   I have some books read.

15   Sue went to the supermarket to some bread.

16   I am busy too to help you.

17   I don't have enough time talk to you.

18   I'm studying hard pass the exam.

19   I was to tired to finish my homework last night.

20   I sometimes go to the café for to get a cup of coffee.

21   It can be fun study math.

22   Sally promised help me with my homework.

23   Can you lend me something for read?

24   I can't go out with you. I have a lot of letters for to write.

25   I'm too tired for finish the work.

B 1번처럼 to부정사를 사용하여 한 문장으로 만드시오.

1 I saw Cathy. I was happy.

I was happy to see Cathy.

2 I found my lost watch. I was glad.

3 I failed the exam. I was sad.

4 We won the baseball game. We were pleased.

5 I helped you with your homework. I was happy.

6 We heard the bad news about Jim. We were surprised.

C 1번처럼 to부정사를 사용하여 한 문장으로 만드시오.

1 Sarah can't go on vacation. She's too busy.

Sarah is too busy to go on vacation.

2 Fred couldn't buy two CDs. He didn't bring enough money.

3 Chris couldn't buy the car. He didn't have enough money.

4 I can't see you tonight. I'm too busy.

5 We can go swimming. It's hot enough.

6 Alicia can't solve the problem. She isn't smart enough.

D   다음 밑줄 친 부분에 가장 적절한 것을 고르시오.

1   My sister is ten years old, so she is _______ drive.
a. too young to
b. old enough to
c. young enough to
d. old enough for

2   I went to the gym _______ some exercise.
a. for do
b. to do
c. do
d. did

3   It isn't difficult _______ this book.
a. understand
b. for understand
c. to understand
d. for to understand

4   Are you ready? It's time _______.
a. for go
b. go
c. must go
d. to go

5   _______ is not easy to learn English.
a. That
b. This
c. It
d. There

6   We were surprised _______ the news.
a. heard
b. to heard
c. to hear
d. hear

7   It wasn't _______ to the beach.
a. too warm go
b. too warm to went
c. enough warm to go
d. warm enough to go

8   This coffee is _______ to drink.
a. sweet too
b. too sweet
c. enough sweet
d. sweetly enough

9   She was happy _______ in Los Angeles.
a. see him
b. to see him
c. to saw him
d. saw him

10   I would like _______ the Statue of Liberty.
a. visit
b. visited
c. to visit
d. visiting

11 I want to go to the concert, but it's difficult _______ a ticket for it.

    a. to get   b. get

    c. got   d. gotten

12 I stopped at the gas station _______ gas.

    a. for get   b. to get

    c. for to get   d. get

13 He wasn't _______ to go windsurfing.

    a. brave   b. brave enough

    c. enough brave   d. very brave

14 Did you have time _______ to Susan?

    a. talk   b. to talk

    c. talks   d. talked

15 Do you have _______ to buy a car?

    a. money enough   b. too money

    c. enough money   d. enough rich

16 I couldn't find my car because it was _______.

    a. dark enough   b. enough dark

    c. too dark   d. dark too

17 We can't play baseball because we don't have _______.

    a. players enough   b. enough players

    c. too players   d. much players

18 We decided _______ on a picnic next week.

    a. go   b. went

    c. to go   d. going

19 Did you find anyone _______ you?

    a. help   b. to help

    c. helped   d. to helped

20 They went to the department store _______ some toys.

    a. buy   b. for buy

    c. for   d. for to buy

Chapter 14

동명사와 분사

Form

동명사 (주어)	동사	보어
Swimming	is	good exercise.
Riding a horse	is	fun.

Meaning & Use

1_ 동명사는 「동사원형＋ing」의 형태로 주어나 목적어 또는 보어로 쓰여 명사 역할을 하는 것을 말한다.

Traveling abroad takes a lot of time. / They enjoy singing.

My hobby is collecting stamps.

2_ 주어로 쓰이는 동명사 구문은 to부정사 구문과 같은 의미를 나타낸다.

Learning math is difficult.

= It is difficult to learn math.

Listening well is an important skill.

= It is an important skill to listen well.

3_ to부정사가 문장의 주어인 경우에 to부정사를 문장 뒤에 두고 원래 주어 자리에 가주어 it을 쓰는 것처럼 동명사가 주어인 경우에도 이러한 용법으로 쓸 수 있지만, 대개 일부 표현으로 한정된다.

It is nice to talk with you.

To talk with you is nice.

Studying for exam is no fun.

It is no fun studying for exams.

Key point_ 동명사 **vs.** 현재분사

학교 내신시험에서는 동명사와 현재분사를 구별하는 문제가 종종 출제된다. 특히, 동명사가 보어로 쓰이는 경우는 현재진행형과 혼동하기 쉬운데, 동명사일 때는 주어와 보어가 똑같은 대상을 나타낸다는 점을 기억하면 구별하기가 쉽다.

My hobby is collecting stamps. (동명사, my hobby = collecting stamps)

She is collecting stamps. (현재분사, She ≠ collecting stamps)

A 동명사를 사용하여 문장을 완성하시오.

1 ______________________ (find / a good job) isn't easy.

2 ______________________ (watch / TV) is the most popular pastime.

3 ______________________ (eat / too much ice cream) is bad for you.

4 ______________________ (join / a club) is a good way to meet new people.

5 ______________________ (shop / on the Internet) saves time and money.

6 ______________________ (exercise / every day) isn't much fun.

7 ______________________ (save / money) is difficult.

B 1, 2번처럼 동명사가 주어인 문장은 to부정사가 주어인 문장으로, to부정사가 주어인 문장은 동명사가 주어인 문장으로 바꾸어 쓰시오.

1 Finishing the work on time is important.
   It is important to finish the work on time.

2 It isn't easy to ride horses.
   Riding horses isn't easy.

3 Playing baseball is fun.
   ____

4 It takes a long time to learn a foreign language.
   ____

5 Being polite to other people is important.
   ____

6 It is dangerous to walk alone at night.
   ____

7 Having good friends is important.
   ____

8 It is good for your health to eat fruit and vegetables.
   ____

Form

주어	동사	동명사 (목적어)
They	**enjoy**	**swimming**.
My father	**stopped**	**smoking**.

Meaning & Use

1_ 13장에서 본 것처럼 to부정사를 목적어로 갖는 동사가 있는 것처럼 동명사를 목적어로 갖는 동사들이 있다.

enjoy	finish	give up	mind	stop

Sophia enjoyed throwing a party.

Would you mind opening the window?

My mother gave up drinking.

2_ stop 다음에 동명사가 올 때와 to부정사가 올 때는 각각 뜻이 다르므로 주의해야 한다. 이 경우 동명사가 stop의 목적어인 데 반해, to부정사는 단지 부사적 용법으로 쓰인 것이기 때문이다.

Thelma stopped smoking. (담배를 끊었다.)

Thelma stopped to smoke. (담배를 피우기 위해 멈추었다.)

Key point_ 목적어로서의 to부정사와 동명사

TOEIC 등의 시험에서는 목적어로 to부정사가 와야 하는지, 동명사가 와야 하는지를 자주 출제한다. 목적어로서의 to부정사가 대개 앞으로 일어날 일을 나타내는 데 반해, 동명사는 대개 이미 일어난 일을 나타낸다는 점을 생각하면 쉽게 문제를 해결할 수 있다.

We decided to buy the most expensive house in the world. (앞으로 일어날 일)

Louise finished doing her homework. (이미 일어난 일)

A 동명사나 to부정사로 문장을 완성하시오.

1 Have they finished ___________ (paint) the house?

2 We've decided ___________ (go) to the beach.

3 We enjoy ___________ (sit) in the garden.

4 I would like ___________ (go) for a walk.

5 Paula gave up ___________ (eat) junk food.

6 Chris enjoys ___________ (spend) time with her children.

7 I don't mind ___________ (get up) early to go to the gym.

8 Can't Amy just stop ___________ (talk) about her sister?

9 Didn't you promise ___________ (take) the children to the zoo?

10 I stopped ___________ (play) tennis.

B 동명사나 to부정사로 대화를 완성하시오.

1 A: Didn't you promise ___________ (study) harder?
   B: Just stop ___________ (tell) me what to do! This is my life!

2 A: At last, I finished ___________ (prepare) for the final.
   B: What do you want ___________ (do) now?

3 A: I really enjoy ___________ (travel) abroad.
   B: So, are you planning ___________ (go) abroad soon?

4 A: Would you like ___________ (go) for a walk?
   B: Has it stopped ___________ (rain)?

5 A: Should we take a taxi to the restaurant?
   B: It's not far from here. I don't mind ___________ (walk).

6 A: I gave up ___________ (try) to fix my car.
   B: So, did you decide ___________ (buy) a new car instead?

Form

	전치사	동명사	
Thank you	**for**	**coming**	to the party.
I am good	**at**	**making**	things.

Meaning & Use

1 _ 전치사란 명사나 대명사 앞(前)에 놓인다(置)고 해서 붙여진 이름이다. at, by, for, from, in, of, to, with와 같은 전치사는 「전치사＋명사/대명사」의 형태로 구(phrase)를 만들어 형용사나 부사의 역할을 한다.

The building <u>on the hill</u> is very old. (The building을 수식: 형용사구)

I went to the park <u>with Jane</u>. (went를 수식: 부사구)

2 _ 전치사의 목적어로 동사가 오는 경우에는 to부정사가 아니라 동명사를 쓰는 것이 원칙이다. 이것은 동명사가 명사적 성격이 더 강하기 때문이다.

She is afraid of losing money.

Thank you for coming to this meeting.

3 _ 다음은 흔히 쓰이는 「전치사＋동명사」표현들이다.

I'm fond of listening to music.

I'm good at playing the guitar.

We're interested in working abroad.

He's thinking about buying a laptop computer.

I'm looking forward to seeing you soon.

Key point _ to부정사 vs. 전치사

TOEIC 등 주요 영어시험에서는 look forward to의 to가 to부정사의 to가 아니라 전치사 to라는 점을 아주 자주 출제한다. 그만큼 혼동하기 쉽다는 점을 감안하여, 다음 예문을 통해 확실하게 익혀두자.

I'm looking forward to hearing from you soon. (O)

I'm looking forward to hear from you soon. (X)

A   주어진 동사를 알맞은 형태로 바꾸어 문장을 완성하시오.

1   Jim is interested in ___________ (become) a flight attendant.

2   Susie is good at ___________ (make) me smile.

3   Thank you for ___________ (help) me with my homework.

4   Matt is fond of ___________ (catch) frogs.

5   They are afraid of ___________ (lose) their jobs.

6   You can make money by ___________ (write) novels.

7   Gertrude is thinking about ___________ (buy) a horse.

B   주어진 동사를 알맞은 형태로 바꾸어 문장을 완성하시오.

1   Are you afraid of ___________ (ride) a bicycle?

2   Thank you for ___________ (give) me good advice.

3   Are you interested in ___________ (work) at a restaurant?

4   Maggie is fond of ___________ (make) fun of her friends.

5   She is good at ___________ (play) chess.

6   We're looking forward to ___________ (go) on a picnic.

7   I'm fond of ___________ (play) video games.

8   John is good at ___________ (make) girls cry.

C   주어진 동사를 알맞은 형태로 바꾸어 문장을 완성하시오.

1   Thanks for _________ (write) to me and for _________ (send) me the books.
    I really enjoyed _________ (read) them, especially *The Old Man and the
    Sea*.

2   I'm interested in ___________ (get) a job at a hotel. I wouldn't mind
    ___________ (work) part-time.

3   Thank you for ___________ (visit) the Student Club webpage. If you are a
    Taylor College student, you are already a member! Now is the time to think
    about ___________ (join) one of our many clubs.

Form

1 I **went shopping** yesterday.

2 I was **busy doing** my homework.

3 I **had a good time camping** last weekend.

Meaning & Use

1_ 동명사가 쓰이는 주요 표현들은 다음과 같다.

- go ~ing: ~하러 가다

  go swimming   go shopping   go fishing   go skiing

  go jogging   go camping   go hiking   go sightseeing

  It's a nice day. Let's go swimming.

- have trouble/difficulty/a hard time ~ing: ~에 어려움을 겪다

  have a good time ~ing: 즐겁게 ~하다

  I had trouble finding Tom's office.

  I had a good time playing chess with Sam.

- spend time ~ing: ~하느라 시간을 보내다

  They spend time camping by the river.

- be busy ~ing: ~하느라 바쁘다

  I'm busy doing my homework.

- It is no use ~ing: ~해도 소용없다

  It is no use worrying about it.

- be worth ~ing: ~할 가치가 있다

  The book is not worth reading.

- can't help ~ing: ~하지 않을 수 없다

  We couldn't help feeling sorry for the poor child.

A   주어진 동사를 to부정사나 동명사로 바꾸어 문장을 완성하시오.

1   Don't spend too much time ___________ (watch) TV.

2   The movie is very good. It's worth ___________ (see).

3   It was a very hot day, so we went ___________ (swim).

4   It was a nice day, so we decided ___________ (go) for a walk.

5   I couldn't help ___________ (laugh) at my mistake.

6   I've been busy ___________ (study) for the exam.

7   Did you have trouble ___________ (find) the post office?

8   It's no use ___________ (cry) over spilt milk.

9   It's very difficult ___________ (get) a high score on the TOEFL test.

B   잘못된 부분을 찾아 올바르게 고쳐 쓰시오.

1   He went to Canada study drawing.

2   Grace is having a hard time to learn Japanese.

3   Stephanie enjoys to spend time with her friends.

4   Susie couldn't help cry for her little brother.

5   We're planning having a surprise party for Xena.

6   Go to university, you need to prepare for several exams.

7   Are you interested in to learn how to dance beautifully?

C   주어진 동사를 to부정사나 동명사로 바꾸어 문장을 완성하시오.

Amy and I went ___________ (camp) last weekend. After putting up our tent, we spent several hours ___________ (walk) along the beach and ___________ (enjoy) ourselves. Then, when we were coming back to our tent, a really funny looking man came over to us. We couldn't help ___________ (laugh). But that was the beginning of a sad story.

Form

1 The party was **boring**, so the children were **bored**.

2 Everyone was **excited** because the game was **exciting**.

Meaning & Use

1_ 분사는 동사원형에 -ing를 붙인 현재분사와 대개 -ed를 붙이는 과거분사로 나뉜다. 현재분사는 진행형에 주로 쓰이고 (3장, 4장 참조), 과거분사는 수동태와 (11장 참조) 현재완료에 (12장 참조) 쓰인다.

He is taking a walk at the park now.

The book was written by Henry James.

He has just finished his homework.

2_ 그러나 동사 중에서 감정을 표현하는 동사들의 현재분사형과 과거분사형은 일반 형용사처럼 보어 또는 명사를 수식하는 용법으로 쓰일 수 있다. 이러한 용법으로 흔히 쓰이는 분사형 형용사들은 다음과 같다.

boring/bored	disappointing/disappointed	
exciting/excited	interesting/interested	shocking/shocked
surprising/surprised	tiring/tired	

The movie was boring, so we were bored.

He had a boring date.

3_ 현재분사는 어떤 대상이 일정한 감정을 불러일으킨다는 뜻을 나타내는 데 반해, 과거분사는 일정한 감정을 갖게 되었음을 나타낸다.

The movie was exciting. → Everybody was excited.

The news was surprising. → We were surprised.

A 둘 중에서 적절한 것을 고르시오.

1 I was very (tiring / tired) at the end of the trip.

2 Were you (disappointing / disappointed) at the movie?

3 His speech was very long and (boring / bored).

4 Visit our (exciting / excited) new store!

5 I just read an (interesting / interested) book about Togo.

6 Were you (surprising / surprised) at the news?

7 We were (shocking / shocked) by the terrible accident.

B 밑줄 친 부분에 적절한 형용사를 보기에서 골라 써 넣으시오.

boring	interesting	surprising	exciting	disappointing
bored	interested	surprised	excited	disappointed

1 I'm very ___________ because I'm going to Sydney next week.

2 Max is ___________ in computer games and often talks about them.

3 I was ___________ because I had nothing to do all day.

4 Everyone was ___________ by a sudden, strange noise.

5 Paul was ___________ with the results and didn't smile at all.

6 The news was so ___________ ; nobody expected it.

C 적절한 것을 골라 문장을 완성하시오.

1 Ann was (boring / bored). She had nothing to do.
   Ann read a (boring / bored) book.

2 I enjoyed our visit to the museum. It was really (interesting / interested).
   I like swimming, but I'm not (interesting / interested) in jogging.

3 I didn't enjoy the movie very much. The story was too (shocking / shocked).
   The whole house was on fire. We were all (shocking / shocked).

4 The first half was good, but the second half wasn't (exciting / excited).
   We were all very (exciting / excited) by the news.

A   잘못된 곳을 고치시오.

1   I enjoy to walk in the park.

2   He went to skate on the lake.

3   She wanted driving me home.

4   You can become rich by work hard.

5   It's important making good friends.

6   We're thinking about spend our vacation in Venice.

7   Save money is important for your future.

8   I called the restaurant for making a reservation.

9   He's interested in become a nurse.

10   Sue enjoyed to smoke cigarettes.

11   You can get there faster by take the train.

12   Jane is having trouble learn English.

13   Maria decided visiting Tokyo next month.

14   I'm too tired for worked now.

15   I'm thinking about send her a birthday gift.

16   Use this key for open the front door.

17   We are all excited about go to Fiji this summer.

18   I'm looking forward to see you soon.

19   I am glad seeing you here in Paris.

20   It is no use to talk about it now.

21   Sue is busy to send e-mails to her customers.

22   Alice dreamed of become a ballerina.

23   We read an interested story about the earth.

24   Are you interesting in learning Japanese?

25   How was the movie? Was it worth to see?

B 동사 travel의 적절한 형태로 아래 문장을 완성하시오.

1 I'm looking forward to ___________ abroad.

2 Janine enjoys ___________ to many different places.

3 I would like ___________ to China.

4 Do you want ___________ across Europe?

5 We finished ___________ around Canada.

6 We can learn a lot by ___________ alone.

7 We planned ___________ to Russia this winter.

8 Michelle promised ___________ with her.

9 We're thinking about ___________ to Singapore.

10 We spent about two weeks ___________ through Africa.

C 적절한 동사의 형태로 다음 글을 완성하시오.

1 We've decided ___________ (get) married. We're thinking about ___________ (throw) a big party. We've always wanted ___________ (do) something special for our wedding. So we're planning ___________ (have) a really, really big party for us. We're going ___________ (live) happily ever after.

2 *Spider-Man III* is worth ___________ (see). It talks about ___________ (do) good things for all people. The movie is also about ___________ (forgive) other people. They may do bad things, but they usually do not want ___________ (hurt) you. So it is no use ___________ (get) angry with them. Just learn to forgive others and do good things. That's the message of this ___________ (interest) movie.

3 I want ___________ (travel) through Africa. I will enjoy ___________ (eat) lots of delicious foods. I will be able ___________ (meet) lots of ___________ (interest) animals. I'm also interested in ___________ (meet) new people. All of them will make my trip an ___________ (excite) one.

D 다음 밑줄 친 부분에 가장 적절한 것을 고르시오.

1 We decided to go _______ with Mom.
  a. shop
  b. shopped
  c. shopping
  d. to shopping

2 _______ every day is good for your health.
  a. Run
  b. Runs
  c. Running
  d. Ran

3 Thank you for _______ me with my homework.
  a. to help
  b. help
  c. helping
  d. helped

4 I'm looking forward _______ Paris.
  a. to visit
  b. visiting
  c. to visiting
  d. visit

5 It's important _______ every day.
  a. exercise
  b. exercised
  c. exercises
  d. to exercise

6 Some people have a talent for _______ foreign languages.
  a. learning
  b. learn
  c. to learn
  d. to learning

7 Marie had trouble _______ how to use her new camera.
  a. to understand
  b. understanding
  c. to understanding
  d. understand

8 Some students go to the library _______ because it is quiet.
  a. to studying
  b. studying
  c. study
  d. to study

9 Orin is good at _______ interesting stories.
  a. make
  b. to make
  c. making
  d. to making

10 It's interesting _______ new countries.
  a. to visit
  b. to visiting
  c. for visiting
  d. visit

11 Many students use the Internet ________ their homework.

a. does | b. did

c. to do | d. done

12 Jane is fond of ________ names.

a. to call | b. calling

c. call | d. called

13 Gina finished ________ the laundry in just ten minutes.

a. to do | b. doing

c. done | d. do

14 My little sister is afraid of ________ in the dark.

a. slept | b. to sleep

c. sleeping | d. for to sleep

15 We couldn't help ________ for Mary.

a. crying | b. to cry

c. cried | d. for to cry

16 We spent almost three hours ________ our homework.

a. to do | b. doing

c. to doing | d. for doing

17 I had a really good time ________ in Europe.

a. to travel | b. to traveling

c. traveling | d. for travel

18 It is no use ________ about it.

a. to worry | b. to worrying

c. for worry | d. worrying

19 It's not worth ________ so much money for concert tickets.

a. paying | b. to pay

c. to paying | d. pay

20 What do you think about ________ in the country?

a. to live | b. living

c. have lived | d. live

Chapter 15

전치사

Form

> 1 The movie starts **at** 10 o'clock.
>
> 2 Keith was born **in** September, 1995.
>
> 3 A meeting will be held **on** Friday.

Meaning & Use

1_ 전치사 at은 구체적인 시각이나 시점을 나타낼 때 쓴다.

at 10 o'clock at noon at midnight

at night at lunchtime at Christmas

I usually leave for school at 7 o'clock.

2_ 전치사 in은 하루의 일부분이나 월, 계절, 연도 등 비교적 긴 시간을 나타낼 때, 또는 '(지금 부터) ~ 후에' 의 뜻을 나타낼 때 쓴다.

in the morning in the afternoon in the evening

in April in 2007 in (the) summer

What do you do in the evening?

I'm going to France in August.

I'll be back in ten minutes.

3_ 전치사 on은 요일, 특정한 날 또는 특정한 날의 아침, 오후 등을 나타낼 때 쓴다.

on Monday on Christmas Day on my birthday on March 4th

We don't go to school on Sundays.

I'll call you on Monday night.

4_ next, last, every, this, that 등이 시간 표현과 함께 쓰이면 전치사는 생략된다.

See you next Tuesday.

Are you going to Tokyo this week?

A 다음 중 적절한 것을 고르시오.

1   I usually get up (at / in / on) 6:00.

2   Summer vacation begins (at / in / on) July 25th.

3   We'll visit Grandpa (at / in / on) Sunday.

4   I'll be in the library (at / in / on) Wednesday evening.

5   Sue got married (at / in / on) Christmas Eve.

6   Can we meet (at / in / on) lunchtime (at / in / on) Friday?

7   A lot of people go camping (at / in / on) the summer.

8   Where were you (at / in / on) Christmas?

B 적절한 전치사를 써 넣고, 전치사가 필요하지 않으면 X표 하시오.

1   We usually get up late ________ Sundays.

2   She was born ________ 8:00 ________ the morning.

3   The street is very quiet ________ night.

4   We have heavy snow ________ the winter.

5   My birthday is ________ December.

6   Shakespeare died ________ 1616.

7   I'm going to Hong Kong ________ next Friday.

C 주어진 단어를 사용하여 다음 대화를 완성하시오.

at	in (twice)	next	on	this

A: What are you going to do __________ Sunday?

B: I'll get up late __________ the afternoon and have a big meal __________ the evening. And I'll watch my favorite show __________ night. That'll be a wonderful day! What about you?

A: I usually go to church __________ Sundays. So nothing special. But I'm going to do something special __________ Sunday.

B: Oh, what are you going to do?

A: I'm gonna visit Egypt! That'll be a lot of fun!

Form

1 I studied **for** two hours.

2 We shouldn't speak **during** the test.

3 I read a book **until** midnight.

4 I must be home **by** seven o'clock.

5 In the summer, we practice **from** 4 **to** 6 in the afternoon.

Meaning & Use

1_ for와 during은 '~ 동안에'의 뜻이지만, for는 구체적인 기간의 길이를 나타내어 「수사＋명사」의 형태가 이어지고, during은 특정한 기간을 나타내어 대개 「the＋명사」의 형태가 이어진다.

I stayed here for three hours.

He went to Vancouver during the vacation.

I slept for twenty minutes during the lesson.

2_ until/till과 by는 '~까지'의 뜻이지만, until/till은 어떤 동작이 그때까지 계속되는 것을 나타내고, by는 동작이 완료되는 것을 나타낸다.

I waited for Bob until seven.

You have to finish your work by seven o'clock.

3_ 동작이 시작되는 시점과 끝나는 시점은 from ... to 또는 from ... until/till로 나타낸다.

He worked from 8:00 to 5:00.

We'll be away from July 18 until August 5.

Key point_ **until vs. by**

TOEIC 등 주요 영어시험에서는 until과 by의 쓰임새를 정확히 구별할 것을 요구하는 문제가 자주 출제된다. until이 반드시 그때까지 계속되어야 함을 나타내는 데 반해, by는 그 전에 끝나도 괜찮지만 그때가 넘어서는 안됨을 나타낸다는 점을 기억하면 혼동을 피할 수 있다.

Please return the book by May 25. (O)

Please return the book until May 25. (X)

A   for 또는 during 중 적절한 것을 써 넣으시오.

1   I'll come and see you ___________ a few minutes.

2   They met ___________ the war.

3   He woke up several times ___________ the night.

4   She studied in the United States ___________ two years.

5   I had a headache ___________ the exam.

6   We visited Tokyo ___________ the holiday.

7   I lived in Los Angeles ___________ three years.

8   The students looked very bored ___________ the class.

B   until 또는 by 중 적절한 것을 써 넣으시오.

1   The books must be returned ___________ April 5.

2   We'll just have to wait for Jack ___________ 6:00.

3   Can you finish painting the room ___________ Christmas?

4   Can I stay ___________ the weekend?

5   I can repair your watch ___________ next Tuesday.

6   The show goes on ___________ 11:30.

7   You must bring it back ___________ June 15.

C   ( ) 안의 내용과 from ... to를 사용하여 문장을 완성하시오.

1   The shop is closed (2~3)

→   *The shop is closed from 2 to 3.*

2   The beach is busy (June ~ August)

→   ____

3   We go to school (Monday ~ Friday)

→   ____

4   He lived in Texas (2001 ~ 2005)

→   ____

Form

> 1 I saw Ann **at** the bus stop.
>
> 2 I live **in** Seoul.
>
> 3 The papers are **on** the floor.

Meaning & Use

1_ at은 장소의 한 지점, 비교적 좁은 장소, 어떤 특정한 목적을 위한 모임 장소를 나타낼 때 쓰인다.

at the bus stop   at the traffic light   at the meeting   at the party

at the station   at a restaurant   at the theater   at Sue's (place)

We met Jane at the party.

＊정관사 the 없이 관용적으로 쓰이는 표현: at work, at home

2_ in은 공간의 내부나 비교적 넓은 장소를 나타낼 때 쓰인다.

in the building   in Canada   in a bank   in the country

"Where's Dave?"   "In the kitchen."

3_ 그 밖에 in은 다음과 같은 표현에 쓰인다.

in the picture   in the newspaper   in a car/taxi   in school

Who is the boy in the picture?

4_ on은 어떤 장소의 표면 위를 나타낼 때 쓰인다.

on the floor   on the wall   on the ceiling

My office is on the third floor.

5_ 그 외에 장소를 나타내는 전치사는 다음과 같다.

above '~ 위의'   between '~ 사이에'   behind '~ 뒤에'   in front of '~ 앞에'

next to '~ 옆에'   over '~ 바로 위에'   under '~ 아래에'

The bank is between the theater and the park.

Exercises

A at, in, on 중 적절한 것을 써 넣으시오.

1 I met Eric _________ the bus stop.

2 We went to the Louvre _________ Paris.

3 We couldn't find a supermarket _________ the street.

4 "Is your father _________ home?" "No, he's _________ work."

5 The letter is _________ the table.

6 Pisa is _________ Italy.

7 "Did your brother get a job?" "No, he's still _________ school."

8 There is a good movie _________ the theater.

9 We went there _________ her car.

10 There are some pictures _________ the wall.

11 The children are lying _________ the grass _________ the park.

12 Does this bus stop _________ the station?

13 I live in an apartment _________ the tenth floor.

14 Mexico is _________ North America.

15 There is a line of people _________ the bus stop.

16 All the cars stopped _________ the red light.

17 I'll see you this evening _________ Sarah's place.

B 적절한 전치사를 골라 문장을 완성하시오.

behind	above	in front of	under	next to	between

1 Birds are flying high _______________ the trees.

2 The mermaid lived deep _______________ the sea.

3 There was a gap _______________ the two walls.

4 The girl hid _______________ the curtain.

5 Alice was too shy to speak _______________ the whole class.

6 I sat down _______________ Mary and looked into her eyes.

Form

1 Do you like traveling **by** train?
2 Did you go to the concert **with** your friends?
3 I saw Bill **among** the people.
4 He jumped **into** the river.
5 I was walking **along** the street.

Meaning & Use

1_ by는 교통수단을 표현할 수 있으며, 이 경우 by 뒤에 관사를 쓰지 않는다.
by car   by bus   by train   by boat   by plane   by bicycle
Let's go by bus.
cf. It's too far to go on foot.   *on foot   '걸어서'

2_ with이 사람과 함께 쓰일 때는 '~와 함께'의 뜻을, 사물과 함께 쓰일 때는 '~을 가지고'의 뜻을 나타낸다. without은 with의 반대인 '~없이'의 뜻을 나타낸다.
I'm going to the zoo with my friends.
Wait for me. Don't go without me.

3_ between은 둘 사이에, among은 셋 이상의 사이에 쓰며 '~사이에(서)'의 뜻을 나타낸다. between은 시간이나 장소를 나타내는 표현과도 함께 쓸 수 있다.
I'll watch the show between five and seven.
Your letter is somewhere among these papers.

4_ into는 '(밖에서) 안으로', out of는 '(안에서) 밖으로'의 뜻을 나타낸다.
They jumped into the pond. / He ran out of the room.

5_ along은 '~을 따라서', across는 '~을 가로질러', through는 '~을 관통하여'의 뜻을 나타낸다.
We walked along the river.
There is a bank across the street.
The Han River runs through Seoul.

A 「by+교통수단」의 표현을 써서 다음 문장을 완성하시오.

1 I drove to Seoul. → I went to Seoul __by car__ .

2 Judy is flying to Toronto. → Judy is going to Toronto __________ .

3 You should take the bus to Boston. → You should go to Boston __________ .

4 We took the train to London. → We went to London __________ .

5 They took a taxi to the hospital. → They went to the hospital __________ .

6 She went to Osaka on a ship. → She went to Osaka __________ .

B 적절한 전치사를 골라 문장을 완성하시오.

with	without	between	among

1 Did you stay alone at a hotel or __________ your friends?

2 I'll be in London __________ June 15 and August 15.

3 I saw a strange face __________ the crowd.

4 We can't live __________ water.

5 Jane shot them __________ a gun.

C 적절한 전치사를 골라 문장을 완성하시오.

along	across (twice)	into	out of

1 Don't walk __________ the street at a red light.

2 Chris jumped __________ the lake and began to swim.

3 The large building stood __________ the road from my house.

4 A young woman ran __________ the house, shouting for help.

5 We didn't have to hurry and walked __________ the beach.

A 잘못된 부분을 바르게 고치시오.

1 I usually get up on 6:00 in the morning.

2 We're going to Canada on May.

3 I'll meet you at Saturday night.

4 We're planning to go on a picnic on this Friday.

5 Susie has left town. She'll be back until Tuesday.

6 I've known Chris during five years.

7 I met a lot of my friends for the summer vacation.

8 You must hand in your report until 5:00.

9 I'll stay in this hotel by the day after tomorrow.

10 We studied at the library from 3:00 by 6:00.

11 Lynda promised to meet me in three o'clock.

12 Are you still at the work?

13 Lincoln was born on February.

14 Have you read the story on the newspaper?

15 My classroom is in the second floor of the building.

16 There's a bridge under the river.

17 Do you go to work on train?

18 I came here in foot because I wanted to get some exercise.

19 They went to London by a taxi.

20 I cut the paper by a pair of scissors.

21 Wait for us. Please don't go with us.

22 I saw Craig between the crowd.

23 I was walking into the street with my dog.

24 The post office is among the bank and the museum.

25 Jack ran out of the car and jumped for the pond.

B 밑줄 친 부분에 적절한 전치사를 써 넣으시오.

at	on	in	for	until	by	from

1 I'm leaving for France _________ Saturday afternoon.

2 We watched TV _________ three hours last night.

3 Carl is in Canada now. He'll be back _________ two months.

4 Everybody slept _________ thirty minutes during the class.

5 The speech contest is going to start _________ 9:00.

6 We should hurry. We have to get to the theater _________ 7:00.

7 The park is really beautiful _________ the fall.

8 I read the newspaper _________ 3:00 to 5:00.

9 I don't usually watch TV _________ Mondays.

10 I waited for Jack at a restaurant _________ 10:00.

11 We lived in Vancouver _________ 1999 to 2004.

12 "How long will you be away?" "_________ Friday."

C 적절한 전치사를 골라 문장을 완성하시오.

at	in	on	between	by	with	without

1 We usually go to school _________ subway.

2 What's _________ that bag?

3 You can open the door _________ this key.

4 There is a space _________ the two walls.

5 I got angry because they went to the zoo _________ me.

6 Mom is still _________ work.

7 The valley is _________ the two mountains.

8 The picture _________ the wall is very interesting.

9 Don't sit _________ the grass. It's wet.

10 I read about the accident _________ the newspaper.

11 Can I get there _________ car?

12 There's a stamp _________ the envelope.

D   다음 밑줄 친 부분에 가장 적절한 것을 고르시오.

1   Susie got married ________ Christmas Eve.
a. at
b. on
c. in
d. during

2   Can you call me ________ lunchtime?
a. at
b. in
c. on
d. for

3   My birthday is ________ April.
a. on
b. in
c. at
d. by

4   Ann had a car accident ________ last Wednesday.
a. in
b. at
c. on
d. 전치사 필요 없음

5   The summer vacation starts ________ July 25th.
a. at
b. on
c. in
d. by

6   I studied at the library from 5:00 ________ 7:00.
a. for
b. at
c. by
d. to

7   I'll be in Sydney ________ Friday.
a. until
b. by
c. at
d. for

8   I slept for 10 minutes ________ his speech.
a. for
b. during
c. until
d. at

9   We're going to Paris ________ next month.
a. 전치사 필요 없음
b. for
c. in
d. on

10   You must return the books to the library ________ Tuesday.
a. until
b. to
c. by
d. during

11 We met Jane _______ a concert last Friday.

a. at   b. for

c. to   d. in

12 We visited the Statue of Liberty _______ New York.

a. at   b. in

c. into   d. on

13 Is there anything interesting _______ the newspaper today?

a. in   b. on

c. at   d. to

14 I usually sit _______ Jane and Sue in class.

a. between   b. among

c. during   d. through

15 Can I get to the airport _______ bus from here?

a. on   b. by

c. in   d. at

16 Do you like your coffee _______ milk?

a. for   b. to

c. with   d. at

17 All my friends left _______ me.

a. at   b. by

c. to   d. without

18 I walked slowly _______ the road for a few minutes.

a. through   b. along

c. until   d. into

19 Albert got _______ the taxi and ran across Oxford Street.

a. into   b. on

c. out of   d. by

20 Joe walked _______ the room and wouldn't let anybody in.

a. into   b. across

c. along   d. through

Chapter 16

접속사

And, But, Or, So

Form

> **1** Max **and** Joe are my best friends.
>
> **2** You may watch TV **or** play video games.
>
> **3** He's handsome, **but** he's not very nice to me.
>
> **4** I needed advice, **so** I wrote to my lawyer.

Meaning & Use

1 _ 접속사는 문장에서 단어와 단어, 구와 구, 절과 절을 연결하는 역할을 한다.

I met *Tom* and *Judy* at the party. (단어와 단어 연결)

You may sit *in this chair* or *in that one*. (구와 구 연결)

Judy is in the hospital now, but *she will get well soon.* (절과 절 연결)

2 _ and는 의미상 비슷한 내용을 연결한다. 두 개의 단어를 연결할 때는 and를 쓰고 세 개 이상을 연결할 때는 마지막 요소 앞에만 and와 쉼표 「,」를 쓰고 다른 요소들 사이에는 쉼표만 쓴다.

We need bread and orange juice.

She is beautiful, smart, and kind.

3 _ but은 의미상 서로 반대되는 내용을 연결한다.

I like Jack, but he doesn't like me.

4 _ or는 '또는' 의 의미로 선택을 나타낸다. and처럼 세 개 이상을 연결할 때는 마지막 요소 앞에만 or와 쉼표 「,」를 쓴다.

Emma's birthday is in July or August.

You can buy one of these bags in black, brown, or blue.

5 _ so는 '그래서' 의 의미로 원인에 대한 결과를 제시한다. 접속사 so 앞에는 대개 쉼표를 쓴다.

We all felt tired, so we went to bed early.

A 밑줄 친 곳에 적절한 접속사를 보기에서 찾아 써 넣으시오.

> and   but   or

1 "What will we have for lunch?" "Bread ________ coffee."
2 I like carrots, ________ I don't like peas.
3 He didn't call me, ________ I got angry at him.
4 Should I go to the party ________ stay home?
5 Was the restaurant expensive ________ cheap?
6 June is beautiful, smart, ________ funny.
7 He called me, took me to a restaurant, ________ gave me flowers.

B 다음 문장의 적절한 곳에 쉼표(,)를 써 넣으시오.

1 I should not drink tea coffee or soda.
2 I need milk bread and sugar.
3 I wanted to see the doctor but I couldn't see her.
4 They were late so they missed the train.
5 I was very cold and I wanted to go home early.

C 밑줄 친 곳에 but과 so중 적절한 것을 써 넣으시오.

1 The movie was very long, ______ it was interesting.
   The movie was very long, ______ we got home late.
2 The restaurant is very expensive, ______ the food was not so good.
   The restaurant is very expensive, ______ only the rich go there.
3 I lost my bag, ______ I went to the police station.
   I lost my bag, ______ I found $10 in my pocket.
4 We wanted to swim, ______ we went to the beach.
   We wanted to swim, ______ the water was too cold.
5 I've got her address, ______ I can write to her.
   I've got her address, ______ I haven't got her phone number.

Form

1. **When** I was ten years old, my father took me to the zoo.
2. **While** I was walking down the road, I met Tom.
3. I'll wait here **until** he comes.

Meaning & Use

1_ 「접속사+주어+동사」의 형태로 하나의 절이 다른 절을 수식하는 부사의 역할을 할 수 있다. 이 때 이 부사절은 종속절에 속하며 종속절의 수식을 받는 절은 주절이라고 한다.

When I went out, it was raining.
　　종속절　　　　　주절

2_ 부사절은 주절의 앞이나 뒤에 올 수 있으며, 주절 앞에 오는 경우에는 부사절 끝에 쉼표 「,」를 써야 한다.

When I went out, it was raining.
= It was raining when I went out.

3_ 때를 나타내는 접속사로는 when '~할 때', while '~하는 동안', before '~하기 전에', after '~한 후에', until '~할 때까지', since '~한 이래로' 등이 있다.

I watched TV while I was having breakfast.

The show will begin before we arrive.

After he graduated, he got a good job.

You must stay in class until you finish your homework.

I've seen a lot of things since I came to Europe.

＊since ~는 주절의 시제가 현재완료형이어야 한다.

4_ during과 while은 다 같이 '~ 동안'의 뜻이지만 during은 전치사로 뒤에 명사가, while은 접속사로 「주어＋동사」가 뒤따른다.

We didn't speak during the lunch hour.

We didn't speak while we were eating.

A 다음의 접속사를 한 번씩만 써서 문장을 완성하시오.

| when | while | until | since | before | after |

1 Always brush your teeth _________ you have a meal.

2 Somebody broke into the house _________ they were sleeping.

3 He has worked here _________ he graduated.

4 Don't drive _________ you're tired.

5 Wait here _________ I come back.

6 Always wash your hands _________ you have a meal.

B before/after를 써서 1번처럼 한 문장으로 고쳐 쓰시오.

1 I have tea. I go to bed. (before)
   I have tea before I go to bed. Before I go to bed, I have tea.

2 I go to bed. I finish my homework. (after)
   ____

3 I listen to music for ten minutes. I start work (before)
   ____

4 We were tired. We visited the museum. (after)
   ____

5 I usually clean my room. My mother comes to visit me. (before)
   ____

C during과 while 중 적절한 것을 써 넣으시오.

1 I fell asleep _________ the movie.

2 I fell asleep _________ I was reading.

3 We don't speak _________ we're eating.

4 We don't speak _________ the meal.

5 What are you going to do _________ the summer vacation?

6 Do you watch TV _________ you're eating dinner?

조건, 이유, 대조의 접속사

Form

> 1 **If** you're too hot, take off your coat.
>
> 2 **Because** she was tired, she went to bed early.
>
> 3 **Although** Peter was tired, he didn't take a rest.

Meaning & Use

1 _ if는 '만일 ~라면' 의 뜻으로 주절의 내용에 대한 조건을 나타낸다.

If it rains, we will get wet.

If it's fine tomorrow, we will go on a picnic.

2 _ because는 '~ 때문에' 의 뜻으로 주절의 내용에 대한 이유를 나타낸다.

We couldn't play tennis because it was raining.

Because I was very tired, I went to bed early.

3 _ although는 '~에도 불구하고' 의 뜻으로 주절의 내용에 대해 대조적인 사실을 나타낸다.

Although he was tired, he didn't go to bed early.

I went to work although I was sick.

4 _ 접속사 when, while, until, since, before, after의 경우와 마찬가지로 if, because, although가 이끄는 종속절이 주절 앞에 오는 경우, 종속절 끝에 쉼표「,」를 쓴다.

He drank water because he was thirsty.

Because he was thirsty, he drank water.

5 _ 어떤 일이 있을 것이라고 확신하는 경우에는 when을 쓰고, 불확실하거나 가정하는 경우에는 if를 쓴다.

When you hear some news, can you call me? (You will hear some news.)

If you hear some news, can you call me? (You might hear some news.)

A if, because, although를 써서 문장을 완성하시오.

1 ____________ it is sunny tomorrow, we'll go hiking.

2 ____________ I was hungry, I ate a lot.

3 ____________ it is very cold, Ann isn't wearing a coat.

4 I'll be disappointed ____________ you don't pass the exam.

5 I didn't eat anything ____________ I was hungry.

6 We didn't play baseball ____________ we were too tired.

B 1번처럼 if를 써서 두 문장을 하나로 만드시오.

1 You work hard. You will succeed.
   If you work hard, you will succeed.

2 You have a concert ticket. You can park here.
   ____

3 You ask him for help. He will help you.
   ____

4 You're too hot. You can take off your coat.
   ____

5 It rains. We will have the party doors.
   ____

C 적절한 것을 골라 문장을 완성하시오.

1 Alice took a taxi (because / so) she was late.

2 Alice was late, (because / so) she took a taxi.

3 Carl passed the exam (because / so) he studied very hard.

4 Carl studied very hard, (because / so) he passed the exam.

5 Cindy went to work (although / but) she was sick.

6 Cindy was sick, (although / but) she went to work.

7 He is very kind to me, (if / but) I don't like him.

8 I don't like him (although / if) he is very kind to me.

Chapter Review

A   잘못된 부분을 바르게 고치시오.

1   When you are in London call us.

2   Amy has never called me, since she moved to Sydney.

3   But she didn't study hard, she passed the exam.

4   I was thirsty, although I didn't drink anything.

5   It's a nice house, and it doesn't have a swimming pool.

6   I am hungry so I didn't have breakfast.

7   We saw Alice since we were waiting for the bus.

8   Do you want to take a walk but have a rest?

9   I suddenly began to feel sick while the exam.

10   Let's wait by it stops raining.

11   It was late and I was tired, because I went to bed.

12   I met a lot of people during I was on vacation in Japan.

13   I've known him after I was 17.

14   So it was too hot, I couldn't sleep.

15   The workers can't go home by the job is finished.

16   The car stopped, but the driver got out.

17   Yesterday I took the subway to work so my car was at the garage.

18   The subway was full, because I couldn't take a seat.

19   I met George during I was shopping.

20   We didn't go out although it was raining.

21   While our stay in Paris, I visited a lot of museums.

22   We're going to play golf when it doesn't rain tomorrow.

23   When I'm late, don't wait for me.

24   If I go shopping, I always buy some bread.

25   Come to the party, but when you can't come, just let us know.

밑줄 친 곳에 적절한 접속사를 찾아 써 넣으시오.

| but | although | so | because | when | if |

1   __________ I studied very hard, I couldn't pass the test.

2   I studied very hard, __________ I couldn't pass the test.

3   __________ it rained a lot, we enjoyed ourselves.

4   It rained a lot, __________ we enjoyed ourselves.

5   __________ they didn't have time, they didn't go for a drive.

6   They didn't have time, __________ they didn't go for a drive.

7   I don't like to travel, __________ I haven't been to many places.

8   __________ I don't like to travel, I haven't been to many places.

9   I'm going shopping now. __________ I come back, we can have lunch.

10   I'm thinking about going out. __________ I go out, I'll let you know.

11   We can go to the beach tomorrow __________ it doesn't rain.

12   __________ I go on a vacation, I always go to the same place.

C   다음의 접속사를 정해진 횟수만큼 써서 문장을 완성하시오.

| although(1) | because(2) | but(2) | if(1) | so(2) | until(2) |

1   I waited __________ Mary was ready.

2   The party was boring, __________ everybody left.

3   The weather was nice, __________ it was a little cold.

4   I helped Erica __________ she was a good friend of mine.

5   __________ the weather is nice, We'll go for a drive to the lake.

6   We couldn't play outdoors __________ it was raining.

7   I usually drive to work, __________ I took the bus this morning.

8   My neighbors were having a party, __________ I couldn't sleep because of the noise.

9   __________ you don't like him, you should be kind to him.

10   You must stay in the office __________ you finish your work.

D 다음 밑줄 친 부분에 가장 적절한 것을 고르시오.

1 _______ he was late, he didn't hurry.

a. Because
b. Although
c. Since
d. After

2 We couldn't go on a picnic _______ it was raining.

a. although
b. until
c. because
d. so

3 The movie was good, _______ it was very popular.

a. because
b. but
c. although
d. so

4 You should see a doctor _______ you don't feel well.

a. if
b. although
c. or
d. so

5 Do you like action movies _______ comedies?

a. but
b. or
c. so
d. before

6 I haven't seen Kate for 3 years _______ she moved to America.

a. until
b. before
c. since
d. after

7 I'll be with you _______ you finish your homework.

a. until
b. but
c. since
d. because

8 Dave was sick, _______ he went to work.

a. so
b. but
c. although
d. or

9 I didn't go to bed early last night _______ I was very tired.

a. but
b. because
c. although
d. when

10 _______ I was sitting on a train, I had an idea.

a. Since
b. Although
c. Because
d. While

11　I often fall asleep _______ the lesson.

a. while　　　　　　　　　　b. during

c. for　　　　　　　　　　　d. without

12　_______ Laura returns, I'll give her your message.

a. Until　　　　　　　　　　b. During

c. Before　　　　　　　　　d. When

13　Would you like a hot drink _______ you go to bed?

a. after　　　　　　　　　　b. while

c. before　　　　　　　　　d. because

14　I spoke very slowly _______ he didn't understand English very well.

a. so　　　　　　　　　　　b. when

c. although　　　　　　　　d. because

15　_______ the train was late, I got there in time.

a. Although　　　　　　　　b. Because

c. But　　　　　　　　　　d. After

16　There was a soccer game, _______ the streets were crowded.

a. because　　　　　　　　b. so

c. although　　　　　　　　d. when

17　The food in this restaurant is delicious, _______ it's cheap.

a. during　　　　　　　　　b. or

c. so　　　　　　　　　　　d. and

18　He's rich, _______ he has an expensive car.

a. but　　　　　　　　　　b. although

c. or　　　　　　　　　　　d. so

19　_______ I do my homework, I listen to music.

a. During　　　　　　　　　b. For

c. While　　　　　　　　　d. Because

20　_______ Ann is younger than Bill, she is taller than he.

a. But　　　　　　　　　　b. And

c. Because　　　　　　　　d. Although

TOP GRAMMAR 초급 – 2
For Beginners

중쇄 펴낸날 ｜ 2011년 7월 20일

지은이 ｜ 채 이 형

펴낸이 ｜ 강 남 현

펴낸곳 ｜ 월드컴출판사

등록 ｜ 2000년 1월 17일

주소 ｜ 서울시 구로구 구로동 222-8

코오롱디지탈타워 빌란트 II 1005호(우편번호 152-848)

전화 ｜ 02)3273-4300(대표)

팩스 ｜ 02)3273-4303

홈페이지 ｜ www.wcbooks.co.kr

이메일 ｜ wc4300@yahoo.co.kr

TOP GRAMMAR

초급 - 2

For Beginners

Workbook

WorldCom

Chapter 9

비교

A 주어진 단어를 사용하여 (not) as ~ as 문장을 만드시오.

1 my brother / not be / tall / me

____

2 you / speak English / well / her

____

3 he / be not / kind / her

____

4 Ellen / work / hard / them

____

5 they / travel / much / us

____

6 math / be / difficult / science

____

7 children / be not / strong / adults

____

B 밑줄 친 곳에 적절한 표현을 넣어 문장을 완성하시오.

bright	cold	kind	strong	blue	dark	white

1 Didn't you turn on the heater? It's too cold in here. My hands are as __________ as ice.

2 Don't be afraid of Jim. He's as __________ as an angel.

3 The city was as __________ as night.

4 Her eyes were as __________ as stars.

5 Their love was as __________ as diamond.

6 Your eyes are as __________ as the sea.

7 Her skin was as __________ as snow.

A 다음 문장을 비교급 구문을 사용하여 다시 쓰시오.

1 I'm 14 years old. You're 15 years old.

I'm _________________________ you.

2 Sue sings well. Betty sings very well.

Betty sings _________________________ Sue.

3 Apples are cheap. Pineapples are expensive.

Pineapples are _________________________ apples.

4 I felt bad yesterday, but today I feel OK.

Today I feel _________________________ yesterday.

5 A soccer player jumps high, but a basketball player jumps very high.

A basketball player jumps _________________________ a soccer player.

6 Yesterday was very hot. Today isn't.

Yesterday was _________________________ today.

B 두 문장의 뜻이 같도록 문장을 완성하시오.

1 The United States is bigger than Korea.

= Korea isn't _________________________ the United States.

2 My friends walk _________________________ me.

= I don't walk as fast as my friends.

3 Tigers are more dangerous than elephants.

= Elephants aren't _________________________ tigers.

4 I write _________________________ Judy.

= Judy doesn't write as well as me.

5 Your apartment is _________________________ mine.

= My apartment isn't as bad as yours.

6 The math exam was easier than the science exam.

= The science exam wasn't _________________________ the math exam.

A 주어진 형용사의 최상급으로 문장을 완성하시오.

1 Dolly is _________________ (young) student in my class.

2 We stayed in _________________ (bad) hotel in the city.

3 Venice is _________________ (beautiful) city in the world.

4 London is _________________ (big) city in England.

5 Judy is _________________ (smart) girl in her class.

6 Kate is _________________ (good) student in the school.

7 Jessica speaks English _________________ (well) in our class.

8 Outback Steakhouse is _________________ (nice) restaurant in this area.

9 The giraffe is _________________ (tall) of all the animals.

10 She's _________________ (popular) student in the class.

11 Lisa is sitting in _________________ (comfortable) chair in the room.

B 다음 최상급 문장을 완성하시오.

1 The South Pole is _________________ (cold) place ______ the world.

2 The turtle is _________________ (slow) ______ all the animals.

3 That was _________________ (easy) question.

4 Ellen is _________________ (good) singer ______ the band.

5 My father is _________________ (tall) man ______ the town.

6 Who is _________________ (old) ______ your three aunts?

7 Mount Elbrus is _________________ (high) mountain ______ Europe.

8 Clara is _________________ (happy) ______ us all.

9 The elephant is _________________ (large) animal on land.

10 I'm _________________ (young) ______ the four children.

11 Diamonds are _________________ (expensive) ______ this store.

Chapter 10

조동사

A   적절한 것을 고르시오.

1   My brother can (play / plays) the violin very well.
2   Could you please (open / opened) the window?
3   What time are you going (get / to get) here?
4   It may (be / is) too cold for a walk.
5   Will you (be / are) at the meeting tomorrow?

B   다음 문장을 부정문으로 바꿔 쓰시오. 가능하면 조동사는 축약하시오.

1   Rob must clean the rest room himself.

____

2   I could run very fast.

____

3   Angela can come to the party tonight.

____

4   Tom should go to bed late.

____

5   Ann may go out tonight.

____

C   다음 문장을 의문문으로 바꿔 쓰시오.

1   Diana can speak Japanese.

____?

2   Jean could read 300 pages a day.

____?

3   She'll be at home tonight.

____?

4   John should do his homework by himself.

____?

5   All visitors must park their cars at the parking lot.

____?

A 문맥에 맞게 can, can't, could, couldn't를 써 넣으시오.

1 Don't shout. I __________ hear you very well.

2 I __________ watch the program last night because I was late.

3 He __________ play yesterday because he was sick.

4 He eats in restaurants every day because he __________ cook.

5 I didn't have a good seat in the concert, so I __________ see the stage very well.

6 She was good at music and she __________ play the piano very well.

B be able to의 적절한 형태로 문장을 완성하시오.

1 I ______________ get a ticket for the concert yesterday.

2 She ______________ have a long vacation next month.

3 We ______________ go windsurfing in Hawaii last weekend.

4 Our friends ______________ go to the movies tomorrow afternoon.

5 Look! I ______________ stand on my head.

6 Alex travels a lot. He ______________ meet a lot of people.

C 문맥에 맞게 can/can't, could/couldn't, will be able to를 써 넣으시오.

1 I like this apartment. I ______________ see the river from the window.

2 It was midnight. We ______________ see anything.

3 My brother is only two. He ______________ read or write.

4 Carl played well, but he ______________ win the game.

5 There was a lot of snow last week, so we ______________ go skiing.

6 I study English every day. I ______________ speak it very well in two years.

A   1번처럼 허락을 구하는 Can I ~? 또는 Could I ~? 의문문을 만드시오.

1   I want another cup of coffee.
   Can/Could I have another cup of coffee, (please)   ?

2   I want to use your printer.
   ____

3   I want to go home early today.
   ____

4   I want to borrow ten dollars from you.
   ____

5   I want to take the last banana.
   ____

6   We want to have a table near the window.
   ____

B   1번처럼 Can I ~? 또는 Could I ~?를 사용하여 다음 대화를 완성하시오.

1   Student: *Can/Could* I go home early?
   Teacher: Yes, of course.

2   Student: ___________ I borrow your calculator?
   Classmate: Certainly.

3   Brother: ___________ I use your computer?
   Sister: Sure.

4   You: ___________ I use your phone?
   Classmate: I'm sorry, but I'm using it myself.

5   Customer: ___________ I have another glass of water?
   Waiter: Certainly, sir.

6   You: ___________ I speak to you for a moment?
   Your boss: Yes, of course.

4. 요청을 나타내는 will, can, would, could

A 요청에 대한 적절한 응답을 고르시오.

1 A: Could you move your bag, please?

B: (Sure. / Yes, I could.)

2 A: Would you help me?

B: (Yes, thanks. / Of course.)

3 A: Can you give me a ride to the office?

B: (I'm sorry, I can't. My car isn't working. / No, I can.)

4 A: Would you help me with my homework?

B: (Yes, I would. / I'd be glad to.)

5 A: Will you get the phone?

B: (Sorry, I can't right now. / No, thanks.)

6 A: Could I borrow your dictionary?

B: (Sure. / I'm sure.)

B 1번을 참고로 주어진 명령문을 정중하게 요청하는 표현으로 바꾸어 쓰시오.

1 Tell me the time.

Would you please tell me the time?

2 Pass me the salt.

Can _______________________?

3 Give me a ride to the subway.

Could _______________________?

4 Hold the elevator.

Will _______________________?

5 Turn off the television.

Can _______________________?

6 Bring me the menu.

Can _______________________?

A 질문에 대한 적절한 응답을 골라 그 기호를 밑줄에 쓰시오.

_______ 1 Do you have to attend the meeting? a. Yes, he did.

_______ 2 Did Tim have to meet his English teacher? b. No, you don't.

_______ 3 Does Mary have to cook dinner? c. Yes, I do.

_______ 4 Do the students have to study hard every day? d. No, they didn't.

_______ 5 Did they have to pay in cash? e. No, she doesn't.

_______ 6 Do we have to introduce ourselves? f. Yes, they do.

B 다음은 학교의 규칙들이다. 1번처럼 must를 사용하여 다시 쓰시오.

1 Come to class on time.
   You must come to class on time.

2 Attend all classes.
   ____

3 Bring your pens and paper.
   ____

4 Respect your teacher.
   ____

5 Do your homework.
   ____

C 1번처럼 have to의 적절한 형태로 문장을 완성하시오.

1 _I have to leave_ (I / leave) now because I have an appointment with
   my doctor.

2 _________________ (Carl / take a taxi) to school because he was late.

3 _________________ (you / work) every weekend?

4 _________________ (Susie / go) to the meeting yesterday?

5 _________________ (I / do) this work now, or can I do it tomorrow?

A must와 mustn't를 써서 문장을 완성하시오.

1 You _______________ stop at red lights.

2 You _______________ drink and drive.

3 You _______________ drive too fast.

4 You _______________ wear your seat belt.

5 You _______________ talk loudly in the library.

6 You _______________ come late to school.

7 You _______________ take a shower before going into the pool.

B mustn't와 don't/doesn't have to를 써서 문장을 완성하시오.

1 Friday is a holiday. I _______________ go to school.

2 You _______________ pay now. You can do it later.

3 Passengers _______________ speak to the driver.

4 In soccer, you _______________ touch the ball with your hands.

5 Angela is on vacation. She _______________ get up early.

6 We _______________ eat in the computer lab.

7 I _______________ buy any milk. I have enough.

C 문맥에 맞게 mustn't와 don't have to를 써 넣으시오.

1 You _______________ drive so fast. The police will stop you.

2 You _______________ drive so fast. We have a lot of time.

3 You _______________ shout. I can hear you very well.

4 You _______________ shout. We must be quiet in the library.

5 We _______________ stop here. This place isn't safe.

6 We _______________ stop here. There's another gas station
on the next corner.

7 You _______________ clean the classroom. It looks clean.

8 You _______________ clean the classroom. The class is not over yet.

A should 또는 shouldn't을 사용하여 다음 문장을 완성하시오.

1 You _____________ play video games every day.

2 Children _____________ eat too many candies.

3 We _____________ go to the dentist twice a year.

4 We _____________ play on the street.

5 You _____________ play with matches.

6 Jason _____________ watch TV all day long.

7 Children _____________ listen to their parents.

B 'd better 또는 'd better not을 사용하여 다음 문장을 완성하시오.

1 Oh, no. My car window is broken. I _______________ call the police.

2 We're late. We _______________ call Mom.

3 We _______________ stay up late. We have an exam tomorrow morning.

4 We're lost. We _______________ ask for directions.

5 I _______________ go out tonight. I have a lot of work to do.

6 You _______________ go out. It's raining.

7 You _______________ see the doctor, or your cold will get worse.

C 주어진 표현과 'd better 또는 'd better not을 사용하여 문장을 완성하시오.

study harder	wash it	see a doctor	touch it
leave a tip	go to the dentist	leave early	

1 Cindy has a toothache. She _______________________________.

2 The car is dirty. I _______________________________.

3 The service is really bad. We _______________________________.

4 My grades are not good. I _______________________________.

5 The traffic will be heavier soon. We _______________________________.

6 The snake is dangerous. We _______________________________.

7 Ann is sick. She _______________________________.

A must 또는 can't를 써서 문장을 완성하시오.

1 The dog is barking. There __________ be someone at the door.

2 We started working just ten minutes ago. You __________ be tired already.

3 It's not very expensive. It __________ be more than ten dollars.

4 You won the first prize. Your parents __________ be proud of you.

5 She's very short. She __________ be taller than seven feet.

6 Hello, you look familiar. You __________ be Bill's father!

7 Peter doesn't speak French, so he __________ be from France.

B may/might, must, can't를 써서 문장을 완성하시오.

1 A: Is Chris Smith a football player?
   B: He __________ be, but I'm not sure.

2 A: I think Ann's brother is in the army.
   B: He __________ be a soldier; he's only sixteen.

3 A: Fred isn't in his room. Where is he?
   B: I don't know. He __________ be at the gym.

4 A: Ellen has a lot of music CDs.
   B: She __________ like music very much.

5 A: We're thinking about going to Paris this summer.
   B: Wow! That __________ be an exciting trip.

6 A: Mr. and Mrs. White are not nice to others.
   B: They __________ have many friends.

7 A: Cindy always wears expensive dresses.
   B: She __________ be poor.

8 A: I called Carl several times, but there was no answer.
   B: He __________ be at home.

9 A: Lisa buys a new dress every day.
   B: She __________ spend a lot of money on clothes.

Chapter 11

수동태

A   주어진 동사의 알맞은 형태로 문장을 완성하시오.

> teach   write   send   use   repair   invent   sing   clean

1   The computer _______________ by Jenny last week.

2   "Let it be" _______________ by the Beatles.

3   E-mails _______________ to the customers by the company every week.

4   The telephone _______________ by Bell.

5   *Romeo and Juliet* _______________ by Shakespeare.

6   Cell phones _______________ by people every day.

7   English _______________ by the teacher three times a week.

8   The classrooms _______________ by the students every day.

B   다음 문장을 수동태로 고치시오.

1   He built the hotel last year.

____

2   Picasso painted these pictures.

____

3   Vincent van Gogh painted *The Potato Eaters*.

____

4   He writes a novel every year.

____

5   I do my homework at the library.

____

6   Our parents visit our grandparents on weekends.

____

7   Tom takes an English test every Friday.

____

A 다음 문장을 수동태로 바꾸어 쓰시오.

1 My mom made a cake for me.

____

2 The police officer helped the old woman.

____

3 The car hit the tree.

____

4 I will clean the place this afternoon.

____

5 Allen takes the children to the concert once a month.

____

6 Andy teaches French in school.

____

B 다음 문장을 수동태로 바꾸어 쓰시오.

1 They will elect a new president.

____

2 She's going to make a dress.

____

3 Amy can fix the machine.

____

4 She may wash the dishes.

____

5 We must clean our rooms.

____

6 They have to discuss the problem.

____

7 We should set the table for our guests.

____

A 다음 문장을 수동태로 바꾸어 쓰시오.

1 June didn't make the dress.

____

2 Sue didn't find the wedding ring.

____

3 Ellen doesn't read newspapers.

____

4 Eve doesn't teach them.

____

5 David didn't write the letter.

____

6 Carl doesn't clean the room.

____

B 다음 문장을 수동태로 바꾸어 쓰시오.

1 Did Allen sell the old car?

____

2 Did Jeff buy a computer?

____

3 Do the boys learn a foreign language?

____

4 Does the store sell foreign cars?

____

5 Did Barbara buy the clothes?

____

6 Did Peter make the robot?

____

7 Do Canadians speak French?

____

A 다음 문장을 수동태로 바꾸고, 가능한 경우 「by＋목적어」를 생략하시오.

1 We saw Brian at the bus stop.

____

2 Someone found these keys in the lobby.

____

3 People know nothing about the singer.

____

4 They sell film at the store.

____

5 They will take the visitors to the hotel.

____

6 They will speak English in the meeting.

____

7 They make these CD players in Japan.

____

8 Someone built this bridge in 1920.

____

9 Many rich people buy the expensive cars.

____

10 They will open a new office in London.

____

11 Someone stole my handbag.

____

12 Someone killed two men last night.

____

Chapter 12

시제 종합 정리

1. 단순시제 vs. 진행형

A 적절한 것을 괄호 안에서 고르시오.

_____ 1 Come to my place right now! We (have, are having) a big party.

_____ 2 We (go, are going) to church on Sundays.

_____ 3 Amy always (is smiling, smiles), but I know her true feelings.

_____ 4 I (am loving, love) James, and we really care about each other.

_____ 5 At the moment, my father (is reading, reads) a newspaper.

_____ 6 Don't worry about us, Mom. We (have, are having) a great time.

_____ 7 I (know, am knowing) everything about Laura.

B 주어진 동사의 과거시제나 과거진행형 중에서 적절한 것으로 문장을 완성하시오.

1 Michelle (come) _____________ in when we were watching our favorite show.

2 Peter (play) _____________ the guitar when his sister entered his room.

3 They (buy) _____________ a large house last year.

4 Michael (be) _____________ born in 1972.

5 At this time yesterday, we (play) _____________ chess.

6 Sarah (drink) _____________ beer when her mother got home from work.

7 The war (begin) _____________ in 1950.

8 We (study) _____________ math when our uncle came to visit us.

9 Clive Sinclair (invent) _____________ the laptop computer in 1987.

10 They (love) _____________ each other, but they couldn't get married.

11 Linda (sleep) _____________ when her mother called.

12 A terrible thing (happen) _____________ last night.

13 Jane (like) _____________ Kevin so much that she would do anything for him.

14 We (enjoy) _____________ ourselves when somebody knocked at the door.

A 주어진 질문의 적절한 응답을 골라 그 기호를 밑줄에 쓰시오.

_____ 1 Where's Isabel?   a. No, she's gone to the concert.

_____ 2 Do you know Karl?   b. No, she hasn't arrived yet.

_____ 3 Are you going to the concert? c. No, I haven't invited her.

_____ 4 Is Jane at the library?   d. No, I haven't met him before.

_____ 5 Is Alice at the meeting?   e. She's gone to the beauty parlor.

_____ 6 Do you want some pizza?   f. Sorry, but I've left my purse at home.

_____ 7 Is Judy coming to the party?   g. No, I have a lot of work to do.

_____ 8 Can I borrow some money?   h. No, thanks. I've just had lunch.

B 주어진 동사의 과거나 현재완료형으로 다음 대화를 완성하시오.

1 A: I _______________ (see) Jason last night.

   B: Oh, really? I _______________ (not / see) him for months.
      How's he doing?

2 A: We _______________ (go) to the concert last Saturday.

   B: _______________ (you / enjoy) it?

   A: Yes, it _______________ (be) wonderful.

3 A: I _______________ (know) Brian for three years.

   B: Really? When _______________ (you / meet) him?

   A: We _______________ (meet) at Jeff's birthday party.

4 A: What _______________ (you / do) last weekend?

   B: I _______________ (watch) TV all day.

5 A: _______________ (you / eat) at Star Restaurant?

   B: Yes, I _______________ (eat) there three times.

6 A: _______________ (be) to Disneyland?

   B: Yes, I _______________ (go) there two years ago.

7 A: I _______________ (never / hear) of this dance group before.
      Are they famous in England?

   B: Yes. They _______________ (be) famous there for years.

8 A: _______________ (you / write) a letter to Betty?

   B: Yes, I _______________ (just / finish) it.

A　주어진 문장과 자연스럽게 연결될 부분을 골라 그 기호를 밑줄에 쓰시오.

_____　**1**　Donna has already finished her homework, so she ___________

_____　**2**　Erica hasn't finished her homework yet, so she ___________

_____　**3**　Tim has just had lunch, so he ___________

_____　**4**　Ann hasn't had lunch yet, so she ___________

_____　**5**　Jeff has finished reading the book, so he ___________

_____　**6**　Sue hasn't read the book yet, so she ___________

> a. may go to bed late.
> b. can't be hungry.
> c. will return it to the library.
> d. may play computer games.
> e. will keep it for several days.
> f. may be hungry.

B　주어진 단어와 already나 yet를 써서 다음 대화를 완성하시오.

1　A: How about some more ice cream?

　　B: No, thanks. I _______________________________. (have enough)

2　A: Is Joe coming to the movies with us?

　　B: No, he _______________________________. (see the movie)

3　A: May I borrow your book?

　　B: I'm sorry. I _______________________________. (finish)

4　A: Is Carl studying now?

　　B: No, he _______________________________. (go to bed)

5　A: Do you know Jason?

　　B: No, we _______________________________. (meet him)

6　A: When are you going to make Amy's birthday cake?

　　B: I _______________________________. (make it)

7　A: Are Dan and Jeff here?

　　B: No, they _______________________________. (arrive)

Chapter 13

부정사

A 주어진 동사의 원형 또는 to부정사 형태를 사용하여 문장을 완성하시오.

1 When are you planning ___________ (leave)?

2 Don't worry. The test may not __________ (be) so difficult.

3 She didn't want __________ (wait) any longer, so she left.

4 They've decided __________ (start) a new company.

5 It's dangerous __________ (drive) on icy roads.

6 She couldn't __________ (reply) because she didn't know the answer.

7 I'm hoping __________ (get) a new bike soon.

8 Tom promised __________ (help) me with my homework.

B 주어진 동사의 to부정사 형태를 사용하여 다음 글을 완성하시오.

take	see	visit	book	buy	go	know

I have an old friend in Sydney, Australia. I promised __________ him. I'm planning __________ there in January. I want __________ about its weather. Do I need __________ a heavy coat? Anyway, I want __________ the plane tickets as soon as possible. Also, I would like __________ a present for him. I really, really want __________ him soon.

C 주어진 동사의 원형 또는 to부정사 형태를 사용하여 문장을 완성하시오.

A: I want __________ (go) on a trip to the beach with some friends this weekend. Do you want __________ (come) with me?

B: That sounds great! When are you planning __________ (leave)?

A: Well, we've decided __________ (start) early in the morning, and I promised __________ (get) to the beach by lunchtime. So, you must __________ (meet) me here at six in the morning.

B: OK, good. I won't __________ (be) late.

A 주어진 동사의 to부정사 형태를 사용하여 문장을 완성하시오.

> think   read   help   wear   go   know   drink   do   buy   talk

1 "Would you like something ___________?" "Yes, please. A cup of coffee."
2 Do you have a lot of work ___________?
3 They gave us some money ___________ some food.
4 Please give me some time ___________ about your plan.
5 I don't have enough time ___________ the newspaper now.
6 I can't do all the work alone. I need somebody ___________ me.
7 I need some new clothes. I don't have anything nice ___________.
8 I saw Lisa at the party, but I didn't have a chance ___________ to her.
9 It's time ___________ to bed.
10 Is there any way ___________ his address?

B 주어진 단어를 사용하여 적절한 문장을 만드시오.

1 I / no friends / to help me / have

____

2 I / some books / want / to read

____

3 It / time / is / to say goodbye

____

4 Those poor people / nothing / have / to eat

____

5 I / to see the band / a chance / have

____

6 I / no way / have / to win the game

____

7 The library / a good place / is / to do your homework

____

A 주어진 표현을 사용하여 문장을 완성하시오.

to buy some stamps	to buy some toys	to cash a check
to learn English	to buy a plane ticket	to eat lunch

1 I went to the department store ___________________.

2 I went to the bank ___________________.

3 I went to the post office ___________________.

4 I went to a fast-food restaurant ___________________.

5 I went to night school ___________________.

6 I went to the travel agency ___________________.

B 주어진 표현을 사용하여 문장을 완성하시오.

happy to have	glad to leave	sad to say
surprised to find	happy to be	pleased to find

Three years ago, I went to the United States to work at a computer company. I was ___________ Korea, but I was very ___________ goodbye to my family and friends.

I was a little afraid of my new life, so I was ___________ no problems living in America. San Diego was beautiful, and I was ___________ friendly people in the office, an interesting job, and a lovely apartment.

Everything went well in America, but I never felt comfortable there, and finally I decided to come back. Today I arrived in Seoul. I was ___________ so many changes, but I am really ___________ here again.

C to 또는 for를 사용하여 문장을 완성하시오.

1 He went outside ___________ some fresh air.

2 Eric went to the library ___________ borrow a book on India.

3 Jane called Alice ___________ some advice.

4 John called the police ___________ tell them about the accident.

5 We use the Internet ___________ find information.

A   주어진 단어와 too 또는 enough을 써서 문장을 완성하시오.

1   This coffee is _______________ to drink. (hot)

2   We didn't have _______________ to buy the tickets. (money)

3   It was _______________ to catch the train. (late)

4   I was _______________ to lift the heavy bag. (strong)

5   I don't have _______________ to talk with you. (time)

6   It was _______________ to go swimming. (cold)

7   She is _______________ to go to school. (young)

8   He is _______________ to reach the ceiling. (tall)

B   too 또는 enough을 사용하여 1번처럼 한 문장으로 만드시오.

1   I can't lift a table. I'm not strong enough.
    I'm not strong enough to lift a table.

2   She can't get married. She is too young.
    ____

3   I couldn't answer the phone. I was too busy.
    ____

4   I can't reach the top shelf. I'm not tall enough.
    ____

5   Ann can solve the problem. She is smart enough.
    ____

6   We can make sandwiches. We have enough bread.
    ____

7   We can buy a car. We have enough money.
    ____

8   Amy can't take the dog for a walk. She is not old enough.
    ____

Chapter 14

동명사와 분사

A 주어진 동사를 써서 동명사로 시작하는 문장을 완성하시오.

| drink | use | speak | learn | stand | eat |

1 ____________ on a chair isn't safe.

2 ____________ enough water is good for your health.

3 ____________ a washing machine isn't difficult.

4 ____________ too much sugar isn't healthy.

5 ____________ is easier than writing.

6 ____________ a foreign language is difficult and takes time.

B 1번처럼 주어진 동사를 동명사 주어와 부정사 주어로 하는 문장을 각각 만드시오.

1 (study one or two hours a day) is important
   Studying one or two hours a day is important.
   It is important to study one or two hours a day.

2 (join a study group) will help you study better
   ____
   ____

3 (meet new people) is a lot of fun
   ____
   ____

4 (learn about other cultures) is interesting
   ____
   ____

5 (fly) is not really dangerous
   ____
   ____

6 (walk quickly 30 minutes a day) is good for your health
   ____
   ____

A 동명사나 부정사로 문장을 완성하시오.

1 Tom enjoyed ____________ (walk) along the beach.

2 Goodbye! I hope ____________ (see) you again soon.

3 I wanted ____________ (read) the book, but I was too tired.

4 I've just finished ____________ (write) the letter.

5 Fred gave up ____________ (try) to find a job in his country.

6 We enjoyed ____________ (have) dinner with Mary.

7 I decided ____________ (learn) French.

8 I stopped ____________ (smoke) last month.

9 He finished ____________ (answer) my question.

10 You will enjoy ____________ (live) in a new country.

11 Carl promised ____________ (study) hard.

12 I want ____________ (live) alone in the country.

B 동명사나 부정사로 문장을 완성하시오.

1 Jason is learning ____________ (play) computer games. He wants ____________ (make) his own games, and he hopes ____________ (become) a famous computer gamer. He would like ____________ (make) a lot of money and travel around the world.

2 Jason's parents would like him ____________ (go) to medical school and become a doctor. He does not enjoy ____________ (listen) to their advice, so they stopped ____________ (advise) him.

3 Jason's sister, Marie, enjoys ____________ (read) the Harry Potter series. She has almost finished ____________ (read) Book 6. She enjoys the Harry Potter movies, but she reads the books more often than she sees the movies. She enjoys the adventures of Harry and his friends.

A 주어진 동사를 알맞은 형태로 바꾸어 문장을 완성하시오.

1 This knife is for ___________ (cut) bread.

2 You can succeed by ___________ (work) hard.

3 Maria is afraid of ___________ (lose) her job.

4 I was able to reach the top shelf by ___________ (stand) on the chair.

5 I ran five miles without ___________ (stop).

6 How about ___________ (play) tennis tomorrow afternoon?

7 We dreamed of ___________ (win) the first prize.

8 Britney is fond of ___________ (use) four-letter words.

B 뜻이 통하도록 자연스럽게 연결될 말을 골라 그 기호를 밑줄에 쓰시오.

_____ 1 Thank you   a. in getting a better job?

_____ 2 She's good   b. about losing my memory.

_____ 3 Are you interested   c. for cleaning the office.

_____ 4 He is looking forward d. to seeing Diane.

_____ 5 I was worried   f. about buying a new car.

_____ 6 I'm afraid   g. at repairing things.

_____ 7 He is thinking   h. of making mistakes.

C 주어진 동사를 알맞은 형태로 바꾸어 문장을 완성하시오.

1 I just joined an international student club, and I'm excited about ___________ (meet) new people. Summer vacation is coming, and some of us are thinking about ___________ (travel) together. I'm also interested in ___________ (work) together to do something great.

2 Many interviewers may ask you, "Do you enjoy ___________ (work) with computers?" Or "Do you mind ___________ (work) overtime and on weekends?" Or "Are you good at ___________ (work) with other people?"

4. 동명사 활용 표현

A 주어진 동사를 알맞은 형태로 바꾸어 문장을 완성하시오.

1 We went ___________ (window-shop) yesterday.

2 He had trouble ___________ (solve) the problem.

3 I was busy ___________ (fix) my broken radio.

4 It is no use ___________ (advise) him.

5 Her ideas are worth ___________ (think) about.

6 I spent an hour ___________ (read) the novel.

7 We are looking forward to ___________ (go) on a picnic.

B 주어진 동사를 to부정사나 동명사로 바꾸어 문장을 완성하시오.

1 Minako is a student at a California state college. She is living in a small town. She enjoys ___________ (live) near farms. She does not enjoy ___________ (study) in a big, noisy city. She is having trouble ___________ (learn) English right now, but has a good time ___________ (talk) with students from many different countries. She was thinking about ___________ (stay) in the United States after graduation, but ___________ (return) to her country seems like a better idea now.

2 I have dreamed about ___________ (run) the marathon. The race is tomorrow. I'm worried, but it's no use ___________ (worry) about it. It's more important ___________ (take) part in it than to win it. I'll have a hard time ___________ (sleep) tonight. But I'll have a lot of time ___________ (rest) after the race. I'm looking forward to ___________ (meet) all the other athletes at 9:00 in the morning.

A 적절한 것을 골라 문장을 완성하시오.

1 Our family is making (exciting / excited) vacation plans.

2 Andy always talks about the same thing. He's really (boring / bored).

3 I'm going to bed early. I've had a (tiring / tired) day.

4 The music was not bad, but I was (disappointing / disappointed).

5 There was a (shocking / shocked) story in the newspaper this morning.

6 We were very (surprising / surprised) at her words.

7 That sounds like a very (interesting / interested) idea!

B 적절한 분사형으로 다음 대화를 완성하시오.

1 A: Can we have a party on Saturday? People won't be (tiring / tired) from work.

B: Sounds great! We need some (exciting / excited) games for the kids. They can be (boring / bored) easily.

A: How about a treasure hunt? The children will be (exciting / excited) about finding candies and toys.

B: Great idea! It will be quite an (interesting / interested) party.

2 A: That was a very (interesting / interested) movie. What do you think?

B: I think it's a little (boring / bored). I'm not so fond of science fiction.

A: Really? What kinds of movies do you enjoy?

B: I like comedies. Have you seen the movie *Home Alone*?

A: Yes, but it wasn't funny. I thought it was (shocking / shocked). I felt a little (disappointing / disappointed).

B: Oh, really? I thought it was very funny.

A: Well, it's a matter of taste.

B: By the way, how about a pizza?

A: Thanks, but it's too late and I'm (tiring / tired).

Chapter 15

전치사

A   at, on, in중 적절한 전치사를 써 넣으시오.

1   I went to Thailand __________ June.

2   Your photos will be ready __________ an hour.

3   It's very cold here __________ night.

4   Let's visit Grandpa __________ the weekend.

5   We can't swim in the lake __________ the winter.

6   I'll see you __________ lunchtime.

7   School starts __________ March 2nd.

B   적절한 전치사를 써 넣고, 전치사가 필요하지 않으면 X표 하시오.

1   I'm going back to New York _____ November.

2   I'm going back to New York _____ this November.

3   I'm playing tennis _____ Friday.

4   I'm playing tennis _____ next Friday.

5   She left _____ the weekend.

6   She left _____ last weekend.

7   We visit our grandparents _____ Sundays.

8   We visit our grandparents _____ every Sunday.

C   적절한 전치사를 써 넣고, 전치사가 필요하지 않으면 X표 하시오.

1   I usually go to Florida _____ December, but _____ last December I couldn't
     get there because I was sick.

2   I always drink two cups of coffee _____ the morning. _____ the afternoon I
     drink green tea. And _____ night I drink hot milk.

3   I gave Jane a present _____ her birthday _____ September _____ this year.

4   We play tennis _____ Wednesdays.

5   The bar is open _____ the evening. It closes _____ midnight.

6   Hurry up! The train leaves _____ ten minutes.

A   for, during, until, by, from, to를 사용하여 문장을 완성하시오.

1   We traveled around England _________ two months last year.

2   I have classes _________ 9:00 _________ 4:00.

3   You can borrow my car, but you must return it _________ Friday.

4   Can you fix the machine _________ tomorrow afternoon?

5   I went to sleep _________ the lesson.

6   I'd like to see you _________ a few minutes.

7   I couldn't sleep _________ the night, so I got up and read a book.

8   I want to stay here _________ next week.

9   It was a great party. We danced _________ six o'clock in the morning.

10   I want to have a sandwich now. I can't wait _________ lunchtime.

11   Adams was a teacher _________ 1999 _________ 2004.

12   Grace will visit London _________ the summer vacation.

13   We've studied English _________ three years.

14   Jackson will be home _________ 6:30.

15   We won't have another vacation _________ next summer.

B   for, during, until, by를 사용하여 문장을 완성하시오.

1   They will finish building the new bridge _________ next June.

2   I can finish the work _________ 5:00 today.

3   Did you take notes _________ the speech?

4   He will stay in Toronto _________ May 5.

5   I've known Renee _________ twenty years.

6   You'll have to be quiet _________ the show.

7   You have to pay the phone bill _________ tomorrow.

8   I have to finish this report _________ Thursday.

9   I will stay in Canada _________ a year.

10   I fell asleep _________ the movie.

A at, in, on 중 가장 적절한 것을 써 넣으시오.

1 Can you meet me ___________ the library this afternoon?

2 Animals can talk ___________ children's stories.

3 Don't leave your keys ___________ your car.

4 She had pictures of pop singers ___________ the wall in her room.

5 "Where's the lemon?" "___________ the refrigerator."

6 Will you be ___________ the party on Saturday?

7 We shouldn't take personal phone calls ___________ work.

8 There's no one ___________ the building.

9 Joe lives ___________ a little village near Toronto.

10 I wrote her address ___________ a piece of paper and put it ___________ my pocket.

11 The cat likes to sleep ___________ the roof of the car.

12 I had a delicious dish ___________ a Chinese restaurant on Park Street.

13 Donna is always quiet ___________ class.

14 Andy got there ___________ a taxi.

15 There's a bug ___________ the ceiling.

16 Is there anything interesting ___________ the newspaper?

17 She has wonderful paintings ___________ the wall.

B 가장 적절한 전치사를 골라 문장을 완성하시오. (단, 한 번만 쓸 것)

over	between	next to	above	in front of	behind

1 Who is that man ___________ Jane? He's too close to her. Tell him to stand in front of or behind her.

2 The gift shop is ___________ the bank and the restaurant.

3 I was walking ___________ a woman, and suddenly she turned around and looked me in the eyes.

4 There's a bridge ___________ the river.

5 The plane is flying high ___________ the buildings.

6 Someone parked ___________ my garage, and I can't get my car out.

A 가장 적절한 전치사를 골라 문장을 완성하시오.

by	with	without	between	among

1 Who is the woman ___________ long hair?

2 Last year, we took a trip ___________ boat.

3 It's cold today. Don't go out ___________ a coat.

4 How long does it take to go to Miami ___________ plane?

5 Are you going there alone or ___________ a friend?

6 The post office is ___________ the bank and the supermarket.

7 Jessica is the smartest ___________ all the girls.

8 It's faster to go ___________ train.

9 They bought a house ___________ a big garden.

10 Max was sick, so I went to the concert ___________ him.

11 We saw a shocking face ___________ the crowd.

12 In the old days, people had to cook ___________ gas or electricity.

B 가장 적절한 전치사를 한 번씩만 써서 문장을 완성하시오.

over	along	across	through	into	out of

1 There was no bridge ___________ the river, so we had to swim ___________ it.

2 I can't see ___________ the window. It's so dirty.

3 He walked ___________ the room and took off his jacket.

4 She took a coin ___________ her purse.

5 Let's walk ___________ the beach.

Chapter 16

접속사

A 밑줄 친 곳에 가장 적절한 접속사를 찾아 써 넣으시오.

and	but	or	so

1 I live in Seoul, ___________ I work in Daejeon.

2 I'm tired, ___________ I'll get some rest.

3 Renee studied very hard, ___________ she failed the test.

4 Last week, John called Ann ___________ bought her a doll.

5 Will Amy go to the concert with Mark, ___________ will she go with Jack?

6 They didn't have much money, ___________ they wanted to eat at an expensive restaurant.

7 We have to eat fruit ___________ vegetables to stay healthy.

8 Do you work better in the morning ___________ at night?

9 Eric graduated last year ___________ started working at a computer company.

10 Do I turn right ___________ left?

B 밑줄 친 곳에 and 또는 or를 써서 문장을 완성하시오.

1 A: Would you like both bread ___________ coffee?
B: Yes, please.

2 A: Would you like tea ___________ coffee?
B: Coffee, please.

3 A: Should we stay here ___________ go out later?
B: Yes, we have to wait until seven o'clock.

4 A: Should we stay here ___________ go out now?
B: We have to stay here.

5 A: Do you want to see both a comedy ___________ an action movie?
B: No, I only have time to see one movie.

6 A: Do you want to see a comedy ___________ an action movie?
B: An action movie.

A 밑줄 친 곳에 가장 적절한 접속사를 찾아 써 넣으시오.

> while   until   since   before   after

1 You should wash your hands ___________ you eat.

2 I'll work hard ___________ my dreams come true.

3 I had a drink with Andy ___________ he left.

4 He won't come back ___________ midnight.

5 Please stay in your seats ___________ the plane stops.

6 I played video games ___________ I finished my homework.

7 Craig has met a lot of people ___________ he came here.

8 I haven't seen my sister ___________ she moved to Seattle.

9 ___________ I was driving down the street, I saw Susan.

10 Carl called ___________ you were out.

B during과 while 중 적절한 것을 써 넣으시오.

1 They got into the house ___________ the night.

2 They got into the house ___________ I was asleep.

3 He got sick ___________ he was traveling.

4 He got sick ___________ the trip.

5 A lot of soldiers were killed ___________ the war.

6 A lot of soldiers were killed ___________ they were fighting.

7 We visited Jane ___________ she was in the hospital.

8 We visited Jane ___________ her stay in the hospital.

9 I fell asleep ___________ his speech.

10 I fell asleep ___________ he was speaking.

3. 조건, 이유, 대조의 접속사

A if, because, although를 써서 문장을 완성하시오.

1 ___________ it was raining, I drove slowly.

2 I got a job ___________ I couldn't speak English well.

3 ___________ you come to Korea, you will see a lot of beautiful buildings.

4 I went out ___________ it was raining hard.

5 Just call me ___________ you need any help.

6 I walked out of the theater ___________ I didn't like the movie.

B 주어진 if절과 연결될 가장 적절한 표현을 골라 그 기호를 밑줄에 쓰시오.

_____ 1 If you don't hurry,	a.	I'll give you twenty dollars.
_____ 2 If you let me use your computer,	b.	it will be much faster.
_____ 3 If you're busy now,	c.	call the front desk.
_____ 4 If you need any help,	d.	you'll miss the plane.
_____ 5 If it doesn't rain tomorrow,	e.	please answer it.
_____ 6 If I'm late tomorrow,	f.	we can talk later.
_____ 7 If we take the subway,	g.	we'll go on a picnic.
_____ 8 If the phone rings,	h.	don't wait for me.

C 뜻이 통하도록 주어진 절과 연결될 절을 골라 그 기호를 밑줄에 쓰시오.

_____ 1 Although it was cold,	a.	but she went shopping.
_____ 2 Amy had a lot of homework,	b.	so she had to take a taxi.
_____ 3 Ann arrived late	c.	he went out without a coat.
_____ 4 Ann missed the last bus,	d.	we had to stop playing the game.
_____ 5 She stayed in the company	e.	because she couldn't catch a taxi.
_____ 6 We had to drink a lot	f.	although her pay was low.
_____ 7 Because it was raining,	g.	although he is a big man.
_____ 8 He doesn't eat much	h	because it was hot.

Workbook

TOP GRAMMAR

초급 – 2
For Beginners

정답 및 해설

WorldCom

Top Grammar

초급-2

정답 및 해설

Chapter 9 _ 비교

EXERCISES

A

1 is not as old as
2 is not as heavy as
3 is as tall as
4 doesn't read as fast as
5 doesn't get up as early as
6 exercises as often as

B

3 Horses are not as big as elephants.
4 Bikes don't run as fast as cars.
5 Spring is not as cold as winter.
6 Chris is as heavy as Holly.
7 Monkeys are not as clever as people.

Workbook

A

1 My brother is not as tall as me.
2 You speak English as well as her.
3 He's (He is) not as kind as her.
4 Ellen works as hard as them.
5 They travel as much as us.
6 Math is as difficult as science.
7 Children are not as strong as adults.

B

1	cold	2	kind	3	dark
4	bright	5	strong	6	blue
7	white				

EXERCISES

A

1	bigger	2	easier
3	thinner	4	more interesting
5	more expensive	6	larger
7	earlier	8	better

B

1	late	2	bad/badly	3	hot
4	happy	5	many/much	6	wide
7	busy	8	fat		

C

1 cheaper than
2 faster than
3 better than
4 more convenient than
5 hotter than
6 heavier than
7 more expensive than
8 smaller than
9 bigger than
10 more comfortable than
11 worse than
12 more interesting than
13 later than
14 thinner than
15 safer than

Workbook

A

1	younger than	2	better than
3	more expensive than	4	better than
5	higher than	6	hotter than

B

1	as big as	2	faster than
3	as dangerous as	4	better than
5	worse than	6	as easy as

EXERCISES

A

1 F-b	2 D-d	3 E-c
4 A-f	5 C-a	6 B-e
7 I-h	8 G-i	9 H-g

B

1 Sue	2 Dave	3 Ann
4 Dave/Fred	5 Fred/Ann	6 Ann

Workbook

A

1 the youngest
2 the worst
3 the most beautiful
4 the biggest
5 the smartest
6 the best
7 (the) best
8 the nicest
9 the tallest
10 the most popular
11 the most comfortable

B

1 he coldest/in   2 the slowest/of
3 the easiest   4 the best/in
5 the tallest/in   6 the oldest/of
7 the highest/in   8 the happiest/of
9 the largest
10 the youngest/of
11 the most expensive/in

Chapter Review

A

1 more older → older
  * old의 비교급은 older이다. more는 2음절 이상의 형용사나 부사의 비교급에 쓰인다.

2 longest → the longest
  * 최상급 앞에는 the를 쓴다.

3 as → than
  * 비교급 형식은 「비교급+than」이다.

4 larger → largest
  * the와 in Korea로 보아 최상급이어야 한다.

5 more → most
  * the와 in the United States로 보아 최상급이어야 한다.

6 biger → bigger
  * 「단모음+단자음」으로 된 형용사의 비교급은 자음을 중복하여 쓴다.

7 easyer → easier
  * -y로 끝나는 형용사의 비교급은 -y를 -i로 바꾸고 -er를 붙인다.

8 more better → better
  * better가 비교급이므로 more는 필요하지 않다.

9 most prettiest → prettiest
  * prettiest가 최상급이므로 most는 필요하지 않다.

10 most early → earliest
  * early의 최상급은 earliest이다.

11 goodest → best
  * good의 비교급, 최상급은 better, best로 불규칙하게 변한다.

12 badder → worse
  * bad의 비교급, 최상급은 worse, worst로 불규칙하게 변한다.

13 the faster → faster
  * 비교급에는 the를 쓰지 않는다.

14 more hot → hotter
  * 단음절어의 비교급은 more를 쓰지 않는다.

15 a most → the most
  * 최상급 앞에는 the를 쓴다.

16 better → best
  * in the class로 보아 최상급이 필요하다.

17 most widest → widest
  * widest가 최상급이므로 most는 필요하지 않다.

B

1 the longest   2 the brightest
3 the most diligent   4 worse than
5 the most quickly   6 funnier than

C

1 oldest / younger / older
2 tallest / shorter / taller
3 fastest / slower / faster

D

2 A football is the largest of the three.
   A football is larger than a baseball.
   A baseball is larger than a golf ball.

3 An elephant is the heaviest of the
   three.
   An elephant is heavier than a
   chimpanzee.
   A chimpanzee is heavier than a rabbit.

4 A monkey is the smartest of the three.
   A monkey is smarter than a dog.
   A dog is smarter than a turtle.

5 A year is the longest of the three.
   A year is longer than a month.
   A month is longer than a week.

E

 1 a   2 b   3 d
 4 c   5 a   6 c
 7 c   8 b   9 c
10 b   11 d   12 c
13 b   14 b   15 d
16 a   17 b   18 c
19 a   20 c

unit 01 조동사의 기본 개념
p.23

EXERCISES
A

1 play   2 pass   3 be
4 may   5 go

B

1 plays   2 x   3 x
4 x   5 x

C

1 Ann can't speak Chinese.
2 Mary mustn't wash her clothes now.
3 Romeo mustn't die.
4 You shouldn't play computer games
   every day.
5 Juliet won't get the best grade in the
   test.

Workbook
A

1 play   2 open   3 get
4 be   5 be

B

1 Rob mustn't clean the rest room
   himself.
2 I couldn't run very fast.
3 Angela can't come to the party tonight.
4 Tom shouldn't go to bed late.
5 Ann may not go out tonight.

C

1 Can Diana speak Japanese?
2 Could Jean read 300 pages a day?
3 Will she be at home tonight?
4 Should John do his homework by
   himself?
5 Must all visitors park their cars at the
   parking lot?

EXERCISES

A

1 couldn't 　 2 Could 　 3 can't
4 can't 　 5 couldn't

B

1 Can David drive his father's car? /
he can.
2 Can Julie play the guitar? / she can't.
3 Can you draw beautiful pictures? /
I can't.
4 Can Susie ride a bicycle? / she can.
5 Can Philip type 50 words a minute? /
he can't.

C

1 will be able to 　 2 was able to
3 was able to 　 4 am able to
5 are able to

Workbook

A

1 can 　 2 couldn't 　 3 couldn't
4 can't 　 5 couldn't 　 6 could

B

1 was able to 　 2 'll [will] be able to
3 were able to 　 4 will be able to
5 'm [am] able to 　 6 's [is] able to

C

1 can 　 2 couldn't
3 can't 　 4 couldn't
5 could 　 6 'll [will] be able to

EXERCISES

A

2 Can/Could I use your pen?
3 Can/Could I have some more coffee?
4 Can/Could I leave early tomorrow?
5 Can/Could I take your picture?
6 Can/Could I borrow your car?

B

1 May I close the window?
2 Can I pay by credit card?
3 Can I watch it?
4 May I sit here?
5 Can I bring my friends?
6 Can I speak to the doctor?

Workbook

A

2 Can/Could I use your printer?
3 Can/Could I go home early today?
4 Can/Could I borrow ten dollars from
you?
5 Can/Could I take the last banana?
6 Can/Could we have a table near the
window?

B

2 Can/Could 　 3 Can/Could
4 Can/Could 　 5 Can/Could
6 Can/Could

EXERCISES

A

1 I'd be glad to.   2 Sure.
3 Sure.   4 Certainly.
5 Sure.   6 I'm sorry, but I can't.

B

2 you please call me back later.
3 you please send an e-mail to Jane
4 you please turn on the lights
5 you please file these reports
6 you please answer the phone

Workbook

A

1 Sure
2 Of course
3 I'm sorry, I can't. My car isn't working.
4 I'd be glad to.
5 Sorry, I can't right now.
6 Sure.

B

2 you please pass me the salt
3 you please give me a ride to the subway
4 you please hold the elevator
5 you please turn off the television
6 you please bring me the menu

EXERCISES

A

1 has to   2 has to   3 have to
4 has to   5 have to

B

2 she has to leave early today
3 I have to go shopping this afternoon
4 we have to take a taxi to school
5 he has to work late today

C

1 had to   2 has to   3 have to
4 has to   5 have to

Workbook

A

1 c   2 a   3 e
4 f   5 d   6 b

B

2 You must attend all classes.
3 You must bring your pens and paper.
4 You must respect your teacher.
5 You must do your homework.

C

2 Carl had to take a taxi
3 Do you have to work
4 Did Susie have to go
5 Do I have to do

EXERCISES

A

1 mustn't   2 must   3 mustn't
4 mustn't   5 must   6 mustn't
7 must

B

1 don't have to   2 doesn't have to
3 mustn't   4 doesn't have to
5 mustn't   6 don't have to
7 don't have to

C

1 mustn't   2 don't have to
3 mustn't   4 don't have to
5 mustn't   6 don't have to
7 don't have to   8 mustn't

Workbook

A

1 must   2 mustn't   3 mustn't
4 must   5 mustn't   6 mustn't
7 must

B

1 don't have to   2 don't have to
3 mustn't   4 mustn't
5 doesn't have to   6 mustn't
7 don't have to

C

1 mustn't   2 don't have to
3 don't have to   4 mustn't
5 mustn't   6 don't have to
7 don't have to   8 mustn't

EXERCISES

A

1 shouldn't   2 should   3 shouldn't
4 should   5 shouldn't   6 shouldn't
7 should

B

1 'd [had] better not drink
2 'd [had] better look for
3 'd [had] better not sit
4 'd [had] better call
5 'd [had] better go
6 'd [had] better not start
7 'd [had] better take

C

1 should   2 must   3 should
4 must   5 should   6 should
7 must

Workbook

A

1 shouldn't   2 shouldn't   3 should
4 shouldn't   5 shouldn't   6 shouldn't
7 should

B

1 'd better   2 'd better
3 'd better not   4 'd better
5 'd better not   6 'd better not
7 'd better

C

1 'd (had) better go to the dentist
2 'd (had) better wash it
3 'd (had) better not leave a tip
4 'd (had) better study harder
5 'd (had) better leave early
6 'd (had) better not touch it
7 'd (had) better see a doctor

EXERCISES

A

1 c	2 g	3 a
4 f	5 d	6 b
7 e		

B

1 must	2 must	3 must/can't
4 can't	5 must	6 can't
7 must		

C

1 may/might	2 must	3 can't
4 may/might	5 can't	6 must

Workbook

A

1 must	2 can't	3 can't
4 must	5 can't	6 must
7 can't		

B

1 may/might	2 can't	3 may/might
4 must	5 must	6 can't
7 can't	8 can'	9 must

Chapter Review

A

1 saw → see
   * 조동사 뒤에는 동사원형을 쓴다.

2 cann't → can't
   * can과 not의 축약형은 can't이다.

3 buys → buy
   * 조동사 뒤에는 동사원형을 쓴다.

4 meets → meet
   * 조동사 뒤에는 동사원형을 쓴다.

5 cans → can
   * 조동사는 인칭에 따라 변하지 않는다.

6 I should → should I
   * 조동사의 의문문은 「조동사+주어」의 형태이다.

7 mayn't → may not
   * may와 not은 축약하지 않는다.

8 please you → you please
   * please는 주어 바로 뒤나 문장 끝에 둔다.

9 have → have to
   * have to = must '~해야 한다'

10 finishes → finish
   * 조동사 뒤에는 동사원형을 쓴다.

11 don't have to → mustn't
   * don't have to는 불필요를, mustn't는 금지를 나타낸다.

12 will → will be
   * be able to = can

13 will can → will be able to
   * 두 조동사는 함께 쓸 수 없다. will이 있으므로 can을 be able to로 써야 한다.

14 will must → will have to
   * 두 조동사는 함께 쓸 수 없다. will이 있으므로 must를 have to로 써야 한다.

15 can't went → couldn't go
   * 과거시제에는 could를, 조동사 뒤에는 동사원형을 쓴다.

16 better → 'd [had] better
   * 'd (had) better '~하는 게 좋겠다'의 의미로 충고나 권고를 나타낸다.

17 don't have → don't have to
   * 불필요는 don't have to를 쓴다.

18 able fix → able to fix
   * be able to+동사원형이어야 한다.

19 not better → better not
   * 'd (had) better 뒤에 not이 온다.

20 must to work → had to work

* 과거시제에는 must를 쓸 수 없고 had to를 써야
   한다.

21 must to drive → must drive

* 조동사 뒤에 동사원형이 온다.

22 has to → have to

* 조동사 Does 뒤에는 동사원형이 온다.

23 maybe → may be

* "~일지도 모른다"는 뜻이므로 "may be"로 나타
   낸다.

24 don't had better → had better not

* had better의 부정은 바로 다음에 not을 붙여
   나타낸다.

25 able to 생략

* couldn't 다음에는 동사원형이 와야 한다.

B

1 c	2 b	3 b
4 d	5 d	6 b
7 c	8 c	9 a
10 a	11 d	12 d
13 a	14 d	15 c
16 d	17 a	18 b
19 b	20 b	21 b
22 b	23 d	24 c
25 c	26 b	27 b
28 c	29 a	30 d

Chapter 11 _ 수동태

unit 01 수동태의 형식과 개념
p.45

EXERCISES

A

1 was broken
2 was written
3 will be opened
4 was driving/was stopped
5 was found
6 will be done
7 invites

B

1 We're [We are] loved by the teacher.
2 The letters are checked by Sue every day.
3 She's [she is] invited to the party by him.
4 The files are kept in the cabinet by Mary.
5 The report was written by Susie.
6 The car was sold by Ted.
7 E-mails were sent to them by us.
8 Nancy was seen at the concert by me.

Workbook

A

1 was repaired	2 was sung
3 are sent	4 was invented
5 was written	6 are used
7 is taught	8 are cleaned

B

1 The hotel was built by him last year.
2 These pictures were painted by Picasso.
3 *The Potato Eaters* was painted by Vincent van Gogh.

4   A novel is written by him every year.
5   My homework is done at the library by me.
6   Our grandparents are visited by our parents on weekends.
7   An English test is taken by Tom every Friday.

EXERCISES

A

1   A test is taken by Fred every week.
2   The phonograph was invented by Edison.
3   The data will be checked by the manager.
4   Juliet is loved by Jason.
5   The homework will be finished by me soon.
6   He was bitten by the dog yesterday.

B

1   A present is going to be given to Mary by me.
2   We may be taught by Mr. Kim.
3   A letter should be written to the customers by Frank.
4   This work must be finished by you by 5:00.
5   The work has to be done by me now.
6   Beautiful pictures can be drawn by Joe.
7   The problem might be solved by Mary.

Workbook

A

1   A cake was made for me by my mom.
2   The old woman was helped by the police officer.
3   The tree was hit by the car.

4   The place will be cleaned by me this afternoon.
5   The children are taken to the concert by Allen once a month.
6   French is taught in school by Andy.

B

1   A new president will be elected by them.
2   A dress is going to be made by her.
3   The machine can be fixed by Amy.
4   The dishes may be washed by her.
5   Our rooms must be cleaned by us.
6   The problem has to be discussed by them.
7   The table should be set for our guests by us.

EXERCISES

A

1   Susie isn't [is not] loved by Bob.
2   This table wasn't [was not] made by me.
3   Many friends aren't [are not] invited to the party by Sue.
4   Tom wasn't [was not] seen at the library by them.
5   E-mails aren't [are not] sent to the customers by the company.
6   The file wasn't [was not] found by Sophia.

B

1 Was Sue met by Ted?
2 Is science taught by Mr. Smith?
3 Was a math exam taken by the students?
4 Is the computer room cleaned by you?
5 Were you invited to the dinner by Ann?
6 Is the report checked by Fred?
7 Was the mail sent to the customer by Joe?

Workbook

A

1 The dress wasn't [was not] made by June.
2 The wedding ring wasn't [was not] found by Sue.
3 Newspapers aren't [are not] read by Ellen.
4 They aren't [are not] taught by Eve.
5 The letter wasn't [was not] written by David.
6 The room isn't [is not] cleaned by Carl.

B

1 Was the old car sold by Allen?
2 Was a computer bought by Jeff?
3 Is a foreign language learned by the boys?
4 Are foreign cars sold by the store?
5 Were the clothes bought by Barbara?
6 Was the robot made by Peter?
7 Is French spoken by Canadians?

unit 04 주의해야 할 수동태
p.51

EXERCISES

A

1 is spoken   2 is borrowed
3 is made   4 are found
5 are cleaned   6 spends

B

1 I'm [I am] paid on the first day of every month.
2 Julie was sent to the Singapore office.
3 A lot of chocolate is eaten in the United States.
4 The telephone was invented by Bell.
5 The tower was built in 1999.

C

1 in   2 by   3 of
4 with   5 with   6 by

Workbook

A

1 Brian was seen at the bus stop.
2 These keys were found in the lobby.
3 Nothing is known about the singer.
4 Film is sold at the store.
5 The visitors will be taken to the hotel.
6 English will be spoken in the meeting.
7 These CD players are made in Japan.
8 This bridge was built in 1920.
9 The expensive cars are bought by many rich people.
10 A new office will be opened in London.
11 My handbag was stolen.
12 Two men were killed last night.

Chapter Review

A

1 at → by
   * 수동태의 행위자는 by로 나타낸다.

2 is → are
   * 수동태의 주어가 복수이므로 be 동사도 복수형을 써야 한다.

3 she → her
   * 수동태의 행위자는 「by+목적격」으로 나타낸다.

4 took → taken
   * 수동태는 「be 동사+과거분사」 형식이다.

5 is → was
   * yesterday로 보아 be 동사는 과거형이어야 한다.

6 is → will be
   * tomorrow로 보아 be 동사는 미래형이어야 한다.

7 finish → finished
   * 수동태는 「be 동사+과거분사」 형식이다.

8 painted → be painted
   * 수동태는 「be 동사+과거분사」 형식이다.

9 buy → be bought
   * concert tickets가 주어이므로 수동태가 되어야 한다.

10 spoken → is spoken
   * 수동태는 「be 동사+과거분사」 형식이다.

11 are → be
   * 조동사 can 뒤에는 be가 쓰여야 한다.

12 by → of
   * be made of '~으로 만들어지다'

13 by → in
   * be interested in '~에 관심이 있다'

14 keep → be kept
   * 주어가 the secret이므로 수동태가 되어야 한다.

15 check → checked
   * 수동태는 「be 동사+과거분사」 형식이다.

16 sent → be sent
   * 수동태는 「be 동사+과거분사」 형식이다.

17 build → built
   * Was ... built로 수동태 의문문이어야 한다.

18 invited → be invited
   * 수동태는 「be 동사+과거분사」 형식이다.

19 rang → rung
   * ring의 과거분사는 rung이다.

20 build → be built
   * A tower가 주어이므로 수동태가 되어야 한다.

21 find → found
   * 수동태는 「be 동사+과거분사」 형식이다.

22 must → had to be
   * must는 과거시제에 사용할 수 없다. 과거시제에는 have to의 과거형을 써야 한다.

23 repaired → be repaired
   * 수동태는 「be 동사+과거분사」 형식이다.

24 sent → be sent
   * 수동태는 「be 동사+과거분사」 형식이다.

25 build → be built
   * a new bridge가 주어이므로 둘 다 수동태가 되어야 한다.

B

1 was painted	2 were held
3 is sold	4 will be taught
5 were killed	6 are paid
7 is grown	8 will be moved

C

1 invented the light bulb / was invented by Thomas Edison

2 made a cake yesterday / was made by Susie yesterday

3 visit the art museum every month / is visited by all the students every month

4 will arrest the thief soon / will be arrested by the police soon

5 will help us next Saturday / will be helped by them next Saturday

6 publish a lot of books every year / are published every year

D

1 c	2 d	3 d
4 b	5 a	6 c
7 c	8 d	9 b
10 a	11 b	12 c
13 c	14 c	15 c
16 c	17 b	18 a
19 c	20 d	

unit 01 단순시제 vs. 진행형
p.59

EXERCISES

A

1 plays	2 are learning
3 laughs	4 moves
5 watch	6 is now talking
7 usually have	

B

1 rang	2 was reading
3 was doing	4 built
5 were playing	6 invented
7 was taking	

C

1 discovered	2 were watching
3 were, doing	4 lost
5 happened	6 visited
7 discovered	

Workbook

A

1 are having	2 go
3 smiles	4 love
5 is reading	6 are having
7 know	

B

1 came	2 was playing
3 bought	4 was
5 were playing	6 was drinking
7 began	8 were studying
9 invented	10 loved
11 was sleeping	12 happened
13 liked	14 were enjoying

unit 02 단순시제 vs. 완료형
p.61

EXERCISES

A

1 have read	2 read
3 has written	4 wrote
5 didn't play	6 has never spoken
7 Have you met	8. Did you meet

B

1 (I) Did you hear	2 (C)
3 (I) were you	4 (C)
5 (I) did you finish	6 (I) graduated
7 (C)	

C

1 finished	2 've [have] been	
3 wrote	4 took	5 ate
6 worked	7 called	

Workbook

A

1 e	2 d	3 g	4 a
5 b	6 h	7 c	8 f

B

1 saw / haven't [have not] seen
2 went / Did you enjoy / was
3 've [have] known / did you meet / met
4 did you do / watched
5 Have you eaten / 've [have] eaten
6 Have you been / went
7 've [have] never heard / 've [have] been
8 Have you written / 've [have] just finished

EXERCISES

A

1 've [have] already met
2 's [has] already gone
3 've [have] already paid
4 's [has] already got up
5 've [have] already made
6 's [has] already left

B

1 already	2 already	3 yet
4 yet	5 already	6 yet

C

2 I've [have] just had
3 I've [have] just called
4 We've [have] just come
5 He's [has] just finished
6 I've [have] just received

Workbook

A

1 d	2 a	3 b	4 f
5 c	6 e		

B

1 've [have] already had enough
2 's [has] already seen the movie
3 haven't [have not] finished it yet
4 's [has] already gone to bed
5 haven't [have not] met him yet
6 've [have] already made it
7 haven't [have not] arrived yet

Chapter Review

A

1 give → given
   * 현재완료는 「has+과거분사」이다.

2 took → taken
   * 현재완료는 「has+과거분사」이다.

3 has → has had
   * for three years로 보아 현재완료이어야 한다.

4 has gone → went
   * three years ago로 보아 과거시제이어야 한다.

5 have you come → did you come
   * When은 과거의 시점을 묻기 때문에 과거시제를 써야 한다.

6 do → have
   * 과거와 현재가 연결되는 내용이므로 현재완료를 쓴다.

7 worked → have worked
   * since가 "~이래로 계속"이라는 뜻이므로 현재완료와 어울려야 한다.

8 has seen never → has never seen
   * 부사 never는 have/has와 과거분사 사이에 온다.

9 lived → have lived
   * since가 "~이래로 계속"이라는 뜻이므로 현재완료와 어울려야 한다.

10 eaten ever → ever eaten
   * ever는 have/has와 과거분사 사이에 쓴다.

11 you've → have you
   * 의문문이므로 조동사 have가 주어 앞에 와야 한다.

12 already → yet
   * 부정문에서 '아직'의 의미로 yet를 쓴다.

13 has → have
   * you와 어울리는 것은 has가 아니라 have이다.

14 have you drunk → did you drink
   * last night으로 보아 과거시제를 써야 한다.

15 Did he gone → Has he gone
   * "그가 파리에 가고 여기 없나요?"의 뜻이므로 현재완료가 적절하다.

16 study → studied
   * 현재완료는 「have+과거분사」이다.

17 Is → Has
   * yet으로 보아 현재완료가 적절하다.

18 know → 've [have] known
   * for half a year라는 기간 표현과는 현재완료를 써야 한다.

19 since → for
 * a long time이라는 기간 표현 앞에서는 for를 쓴다.

20 He's → He
 * he moved로 보아 현재와 관련 없는 과거의 사실
   을 표현하고 있으므로 과거시제를 써야 한다.

21 Have arrived Jane and her husband?
   → Have Jane and her husband arrived?
 * 현재완료의 의문문은 have/has 조동사만 주어
   앞에 놓인다.

22 be → been
 * 현재완료는 「have+과거분사」이다.

23 lose → lost
 * 현재완료는 「have+과거분사」이다

24 have you lost → did you lose
 * When은 과거의 시점을 묻기 때문에 과거시제를
   써야 한다.

25 did → have
 * 현재완료는 「have+과거분사」이다.

B

| 1 already | 2 already | 3 yet |
| 4 just now | 5 just now | 6 yet |

C

1 've [have] bought
2 've [have] found
3 've [have] passed
4 's [has] just gone
5 've [have] never tried
6 's [has] already started

D

1 b	2 a	3 d
4 c	5 b	6 c
7 b	8 c	9 b
10 a	11 d	12 c
13 a	14 c	15 c
16 a	17 a	18 d
19 c	20 b	

unit 01 명사적 용법
p.75

EXERCISES

A

| 1 to | 2 X | 3 to |
| 4 X | 5 to | 6 to |

B

| 1 to have | 2 buy | 3 to visit |
| 4 to come | 5 to see | 6 repair |

C

2 It is important to tell the truth.
3 It is fun to meet new people.
4 It is hard to master breakdancing.
5 It is interesting to travel to new
  countries.

Workbook

A

1 to leave	2 be	3 to wait
4 to start	5 to drive	6 reply
7 to get	8 to help	

B

1 to visit	2 to go	3 to know
4 to take	5 to book	6 to buy
7 to see		

C

to go / to come / to leave / to start / to get
/ meet / be

EXERCISES

A

1 stories to tell 2 homework to do
3 letters to send 4 video to watch
5 friend to meet 6 money to lend

B

1 to take 2 to enter 3 to see
4 to learn 5 to win 6 to go

C

1 to wear 2 to do 3 to talk with
4 to love 5 to help 6 to carry

Workbook

A

1 to drink 2 to do 3 to buy
4 to think 5 to read 6 to help
7 to wear 8 to talk 9 to go
10 to know

B

1 I have no friends to help me.
2 I want some books to read.
3 It is time to say good-bye.
4 Those poor people have nothing to eat.
5 I have a chance to see the band.
6 I have no way to win the game.
7 The library is a good place to do your
   homework.

EXERCISES

A

1 sad to see 2 surprised to see
3 glad to get 4 pleased to eat
5 happy to watch

B

1 c 2 e 3 f 4 a
5 g 6 b 7 d

C

1 to 2 to 3 for 4 for
5 to 6 to 7 for

Workbook

A

1 to buy some toys
2 to cash a check
3 to buy some stamps
4 to eat lunch
5 to learn English
6 to buy a plane ticket

B

glad to leave / sad to say / happy to have /
pleased to find / surprised to find / happy
to be

C

1 for 2 to 3 for
4 to 5 to

EXERCISES

A

1 too	2 enough	3 enough
4 too	5 enough	6 too

B

2 I am too weak to carry the big bag.
3 We were too tired to walk home.
4 I was too hungry to do anything.
5 I felt too sad to talk to anyone.

C

2 Dan is smart enough to pass the exam.
3 Alex is tall enough to play basketball.
4 I have enough money to go on vacation.
5 Lucy didn't have enough money to pay
  the bill.

Workbook

A

1 too hot	2 enough money
3 too late	4 strong enough
5 enough time	6 too cold
7 too young	8 tall enough

B

2 She is too young to get married.
3 I was too busy to answer the phone.
4 I'm not tall enough to reach the top
  shelf.
5 Ann is smart enough to solve the
  problem.
6 We have enough bread to make
  sandwiches.
7 We have enough money to buy a car.
8 Amy is not old enough to take the dog
  for a walk.

Chapter Review

A

1 buy → to buy
  * decide 뒤에는 to부정사가 와야 한다.
2 Is → It is
  * 진주어인 to부정사를 가리키는 가주어 it이 필요하다.
3 for do → to do
  * '~하기 위하여'의 의미는 to부정사로 표현한다.
4 watch → to watch
  * want 뒤에는 부정사가 와야 한다.
5 for see → to see
  * '~하기 위하여'의 의미는 to부정사로 표현한다.
6 to visited → to visit
  * to부정사의 형태는 「to+동사원형」이다.
7 say → to say
  * 진주어인 to부정사형이 필요하다.
8 see → to see
  * would like 뒤에는 to부정사가 온다.
9 That → It
  * 가주어는 it으로 표현한다.
10 enough old → old enough
  * enough은 형용사 뒤에 온다.
11 money enough → enough money
  * enough은 명사 앞에 온다.
12 enough → too
  * 내용으로 보아 too ~ to … 구문이 자연스럽다.
13 see → to see
  * glad의 이유를 나타내는 to부정사의 부사적 용법
    이다.
14 read → to read
  * books를 뒤에서 수식하는 to부정사의 형용사적
    용법이다.
15 to → for
  * '~을 위하여'의 의미를 나타낼 때 대상이 명사인
    경우엔 for를 쓴다.
16 busy too → too busy
  * too는 형용사 앞에 온다.
17 talk → to talk
  * 명사 time을 뒤에서 수식하는 to부정사의 형용사
    적 용법이다.
18 pass → to pass
  * '~하기 위하여'의 의미는 to부정사로 표현한다.
19 to → too
  * 「too+형용사+to부정사」에서 형용사 앞에 to가
    아니라 too가 와야 함에 유의해야 한다.

20 for to get → to get
  * '～하기 위하여'의 의미는 to부정사로 표현한다.
    for는 뒤에 명사가 올 때 쓴다.

21 study → to study
  * 진주어인 to부정사가 필요하다.

22 help → to help
  * promise 뒤에는 to부정사가 온다.

23 for read → to read
  * something을 뒤에서 수식하는 to부정사의 형용사
    적 용법이다.

24 for to write → to write
  * 명사를 뒤에서 수식하는 것은 to부정사의 형태가
    되어야 한다.

25 for finish → to finish
  * 「too＋형용사＋to부정사」형식이 되어야 한다.

B

2 I was glad to find my lost watch.
3 I was sad to fail the exam.
4 We were pleased to win the baseball
   game.
5 I was happy to help you with your
   homework.
6 We were surprised to hear the bad
   news about Jim.

C

2 Fred didn't bring enough money to buy
   two CDs.
3 Chris didn't have enough money to buy
   the car.
4 I'm too busy to see you tonight.
5 It's hot enough to go swimming.
6 Alicia isn't smart enough to solve the
   problem.

D

1 a	2 b	3 c
4 d	5 c	6 c
7 d	8 b	9 b
10 c	11 a	12 b
13 b	14 b	15 c
16 c	17 b	18 c
19 b	20 c	

unit 01 주어로 쓰이는 동명사
p.89

EXERCISES

A

1 Finding a good job
2 Watching TV
3 Eating too much ice cream
4 Joining a club
5 Shopping on the Internet
6 Exercising every day
7 Saving money

B

3 It is fun to play baseball.
4 Learning a foreign language takes a
   long time.
5 It is important to be polite to other
   people.
6 Walking alone at night is dangerous.
7 It is important to have good friends.
8 Eating fruit and vegetables is good for
   your health.

Workbook

A

| 1 Standing | 2 Drinking | 3 Using |
| 4 Eating | 5 Speaking | 6 Learning |

B

2 – Joining a study group will help you
     study better.
   – It will help you study better to join a
     study group.
3 – Meeting new people is a lot of fun.
   – It is a lot of fun to meet new people.
4 – Learning about other cultures is
     interesting.
   – It is interesting to learn about other
     cultures.

5 – Flying is not really dangerous.
– It is not really dangerous to fly.
6 – Walking quickly 30 minutes a day is good for your health.
– It is good for your health to walk quickly 30 minutes a day.

unit 02 동사의 목적어로 쓰이는 동명사
p.91

EXERCISES

A

1 painting 2 to go 3 sitting
4 to go 5 eating 6 spending
7 getting up 8 talking 9 to take
10 playing

B

1 to study / telling 2 preparing / to do
3 traveling / to go 4 to go / raining
5 walking 6 trying / to buy

Workbook

A

1 walking 2 to see 3 to read
4 writing 5 trying 6 having
7 to learn 8 smoking 9 answering
10 living 11 to study 12 to live

B

1 to play / to make / to become / to make
2 to go / listening / advising
3 reading / reading

unit 03 전치사의 목적어로 쓰이는 동명사
p.93

EXERCISES

A

1 becoming 2 making 3 helping
4 catching 5 losing 6 writing
7 buying

B

1 riding 2 giving 3 working
4 making 5 playing 6 going
7 playing 8 making

C

1 writing / sending / reading
2 getting / working
3 visiting / joining

Workbook

A

1 cutting 2 working 3 losing
4 standing 5 stopping 6 playing
7 winning 8 using

B

1 c 2 g 3 a 4 d
5 b 6 h 7 f

C

1 meeting / traveling / working
2 working / working / working

unit 04 동명사 활용 표현
p.95

EXERCISES

A

1 watching　2 seeing　3 swimming
4 to go　5 laughing　6 studying
7 finding　8 crying　9 to get

B

1 study → to study
2 to learn → learning
3 to spend → spending
4 cry → crying
5 having → to have
6 Go → To go
7 to learn → learning

C

camping / walking / enjoying / laughing

Workbook

A

1 window-shopping　2 solving
3 fixing　4 advising
5 thinking　6 reading
7 going

B

1 living / studying / learning / talking /
staying / returning
2 running / worrying / to take / sleeping /
to rest / meeting

unit 05 분사
p.97

EXERCISES

A

1 tired　2 disappointed
3 boring　4 exciting
5 interesting　6 surprised
7 shocked

B

1 excited　2 interested
3 bored　4 surprised
5 disappointed　6 surprising

C

1 bored / boring
2 interesting / interested
3 shocking / shocked
4 exciting / excited

Workbook

A

1 exciting　2 boring　3 tiring
4 disappointed　5 shocking
6 surprised　7 interesting

B

1 tired / exciting / bored / excited /
interesting
2 interesting / boring / shocking /
disappointed / tired

Chapter Review

A

1 to walk → walking
 * enjoy 뒤에 동명사가 온다.

2 to skate → skating
 * 「go+-ing」 '～하러 가다'

3 driving → to drive
 * want의 목적어로는 to부정사가 온다.

4 work → working
 * 전치사 뒤에 동명사가 온다.

5 making → to make
 * 진주어이므로 to부정사 형태가 되어야 한다.

6 spend → spending
 * 전치사 뒤에 동명사가 온다.

7 Save → Saving
 * 주어 자리이므로 동명사가 와야 한다.

8 for making → to make
 * '～하기 위하여'의 뜻으로 to부정사의 부사적
  용법이다.

9 become → becoming
 * 전치사 뒤에 동명사가 온다.

10 to smoke → smoking
 * enjoy 뒤에 동명사가 온다.

11 take → taking
 * 전치사 뒤에 동명사가 온다.

12 learn → learning
 * have trouble+동명사

13 visiting → to visit
 * decide의 목적어로 to부정사가 온다.

14 for worked → to work
 * too ~ to 용법이다.

15 send → sending
 * 전치사 뒤에 동명사가 온다.

16 for open → to open
 * '～하기 위하여'의 뜻으로 to부정사의 부사적 용법
  이다.

17 go → going
 * 전치사 뒤에 동명사가 온다.

18 see → seeing
 * 전치사 뒤에 뒤에 동명사가 온다.

19 seeing → to see
 * glad의 원인을 표현하는 to부정사가 필요하다.

20 to talk → talking
 * It is no use+동명사 '～해도 소용 없다'

21 to send → sending
 * busy+동명사

22 become → becoming
 * 전치사 뒤에 동명사가 온다.

23 interested → interesting
 * 어떤 감정을 불러일으키는 경우이므로 현재분사형
  이어야 한다.

24 interesting → interested
 * 어떤 대상으로 인하여 감정의 변화를 느끼는 경우
  이므로 과거분사형이어야 한다.

25 to see → seeing
 * worth+동명사

B

1 traveling	2 traveling	3 to travel
4 to travel	5 traveling	6 traveling
7 to travel	8 to travel	
9 traveling	10 traveling	

C

1 to get / throwing / to do / to have /
 to live
2 seeing / doing / forgiving / to hurt /
 getting / interesting
3 to travel / eating / to meet / interesting /
 meeting / exciting

D

1 c	2 c	3 c
4 c	5 d	6 a
7 b	8 d	9 c
10 a	11 c	12 b
13 b	14 c	15 a
16 b	17 c	18 d
19 a	20 b	

EXERCISES

A

1 at	2 on	3 on	4 on
5 on	6 at / on	7 in	8 at

B

1 on	2 at / in	3 at	4 in
5 in	6 in	7 X	

C

this / in / in / at / on / next

Workbook

A

1 in	2 in	3 at	4 on
5 in	6 at	7 on	

B

1 in	2 X	3 on	4 X
5 on	6 X	7 on	8 X

C

1 in / X	2 in / In / at
3 on / in / X	4 on
5 in / at	6 in

EXERCISES

A

1 for	2 during	3 during
4 for	5 during	6 during
7 for	8 during	

B

1 by	2 until	3 by	4 until
5 by	6 until	7 by	

C

2 The beach is busy from June to August.
3 We go to school from Monday to Friday.
4 He lived in Texas from 2001 to 2005.

Workbook

A

1 for	2 from / to [until]	3 by
4 by	5 during	6 for
7 during	8 until	9 until
10 until	11 from / to [until]	12 during
13 for	14 by	15 until

B

1 by	2 by	3 during	4 until
5 for	6 during	7 by	8 by
9 for	10 during		

EXERCISES

A

1 at	2 in	3 on
4 at / at	5 on	6 in
7 in	8 at	9 in
10 on	11 on / in	12 at
13 on	14 in	15 at
16 at	17 at	

B

1 above	2 under	3 between
4 behind	5 in front of	6 next to

Workbook

A

1 at	2 in	3 in	4 on
5 In	6 at	7 at	8 in
9 in	10 on, in	11 on	12 at
13 in	14 in	15 on	16 in
17 on			

B

1 next to	2 between	3 behind
4 over	5 above	6 in front of

EXERCISES

A

2 by plane	3 by bus	4 by train
5 by taxi	6 by ship	

B

1 with	2 between	3 among
4 without	5 with	

C

1 across	2 into	3 across
4 out of	5 along	

Workbook

A

1 with	2 by	3 without
4 by	5 with	6 between
7 among	8 by	9 with
10 without	11 among	12 without

B

1 over, across	2 through	3 into
4 out of	5 along	

Chapter Review

A

1 on → at
   * at+시각

2 on → in
   * in+월

3 at → on
   * on+요일

4 on 생략
   * this 뒤에 시간 표현이 오면 전치사가 생략된다.

5 until → by
   * 완료되는 시점은 by로 표현한다.

6 during → for
   * 수사와 함께 쓰인 기간 표현은 for를 쓴다.

7 for → during
   * 특정한 기간은 for로 표현한다.

8 until → by
   * 완료되는 시점은 by로 표현한다.

9 by → until
   * 계속되는 동작은 until로 표현한다.

10 by → to / until
   * from ~ to/until '~부터 ~까지'

11 in → at
   * at+시각

12 at the work → at work
   * at work, at home은 관사 없이 쓰인다.

13 on → in
   * in+월

14 on → in
   * 인쇄물로 된 것은 in을 쓴다.

15 in → on
   * 표면을 나타낼 때는 on을 쓴다.

16 under → over
   * '~위의' 뜻은 over이다.

17 on train → by train
   * by+교통수단

18 in → on
   * '걸어서' 는 on foot이다.

19 by a taxi → by taxi
   * by+교통수단

20 by → with
   * '~을 가지고' 는 with로 표현한다.

21 with → without
   * 논리적으로 '~없이' 의 의미가 적절하다.

22 between → among
   * '3개 이상에서' 의 의미는 among을 쓴다.

23 into → along / across
   * '길을 따라서 / 횡단하여' 의 뜻은 along / across 로 표현한다.

24 among → between
   * 둘 사이이므로 between를 써야 한다.

25 for → into
   * '안으로' 라는 방향을 나타내려면 into를 써야 한다.

B

1 on	2 for	3 in
4 for	5 at	6 by
7 in	8 from	9 on
10 until	11 from	12 Until

C

1 by	2 in	3 with
4 between	5 without	6 at
7 between	8 on	9 on
10 in	11 by	12 on

D

1 b	2 a	3 b
4 d	5 b	6 d
7 a	8 b	9 a
10 c	11 a	12 b
13 a	14 a	15 b
16 c	17 d	18 b
19 c	20 a	

unit 01 And, But, Or, So
p.119

EXERCISES

A

1 and	2 but	3 and	4 or
5 or	6 and	7 and	

B

1 I should not drink tea, coffee, or soda.
2 I need milk, bread, and sugar.
3 I wanted to see the doctor, but I couldn't see her.
4 They were late, so they missed the train.
5 I was very cold, and I wanted to go home early.

C

1 but / so   2 but / so
3 so / but   4 so / but
5 so / but

Workbook

A

1 but	2 so	3 but	4 and
5 or	6 but	7 and	8 or
9 and	10 or		

B

1 and	2 or	3 and	4 or
5 and	6 or		

unit 02 시간의 접속사
p.121

EXERCISES

A

1 after	2 while	3 since
4 when	5 until	6 before

B

2 – I go to bed after I finish my homework.
  – After I finish my homework, I go to bed.
3 – I listen to music for ten minutes before I start work.
  – Before I start work, I listen to music for ten minutes.
4 – We were tired after we visited the museum.
  – After we visited the museum, we were tired.
5 – I usually clean my room before my mother comes to visit me.
  – Before my mother comes to visit me, I usually clean my room.

C

1 during	2 while	3 while
4 during	5 during	6 while

Workbook

A

1 before	2 until	3 before
4 until	5 until	6 after
7 since	8 since	9 While
10 while		

B

1 during	2 while	3 while
4 during	5 during	6 while
7 while	8 during	9 during
10 while		

EXERCISES

A

1 If	2 Because	3 Although
4 if	5 although	6 because

B

2 If you have a concert ticket, you can park here.

3 If you ask him for help, he will help you.

4 If you're too hot, you can take off your coat.

5 If it rains, we will have the party indoors.

C

1 because	2 so	3 because
4 so	5 although	6 but
7 but	8 although	

Workbook

A

1 Because	2 although	3 If
4 although	5 if	6 because

B

1 d	2 a	3 f	4 c
5 g	6 h	7 b	8 e

C

1 c	2 a	3 e	4 b
5 f	6 h	7 d	8 g

Chapter Review

A

1 ~ London call → ~ London, call
 * 종속절이 주절 앞에 오면 쉼표를 써야 한다.

2 ~ weekend, since → ~ weekend since
 * 종속절이 주절 뒤에 오면 쉼표를 쓰지 않는다.

3 But → Although / Though / Even though
 * but은 종속절과 주절을 연결하지 못한다.

4 although → but
 = Although I was thirsty, I didn't drink anything.

5 and → but
 * 상반된 내용을 연결하는 접속사가 필요하다.

6 so → because
 * 이유를 표현하는 접속사가 필요하다.

7 since → while
 * 진행형 구문과는 while이 적합하다.

8 but → or
 * 선택의 접속사가 필요하다.

9 while → during
 * 명사 앞이므로 접속사가 아닌 전치사가 필요하다.

10 by → until / till
 * 절을 이끄는 접속사가 필요하다.

11 because → so
 * 내용상 결과를 나타내는 접속사가 필요하다.

12 during → while / when
 * 절을 이끄는 접속사가 필요하다.

13 after → since
 * 주절의 현재완료형과 어울리는 것은 since이다.

14 So → Because
 * 이유를 표현하는 접속사가 필요하다.

15 by → until / till
 * "~할 때까지"라는 뜻의 접속사를 써야 한다.

16 but → and
 * 동작의 연속이므로 and가 적절하다.

17 so → because
 * 이유를 나타내는 접속사가 필요하다.

18 because → so
 * 결과를 나타내는 접속사가 필요하다.

19 during → while / when
 * 절을 이끄는 접속사가 필요하다.

20 although → because
 * 나가지 않은 이유를 나타내는 접속사가 필요하다.

21 While → During
  * 주어와 동사가 없으므로 접속사가 아닌 전치사가 필
    요하다.

22 when → if
  * 어떤 사실을 가정할 때는 if를 쓴다.

23 When → If
  * 어떤 사실을 가정할 때는 if를 쓴다.

24 If → When
  * 확실한 사실을 말할 때는 when을 쓴다.

25 when → if
  * 어떤 사실을 가정할 때는 if를 쓴다.

B

1 Although	2 but
3 Although	4 but
5 Because	6 so
7 so	8 Because
9 When	10 If
11 if	12 When

C

1 until	2 so	3 but
4 because	5 If	6 because
7 but	8 so	9 Although
10 until		

D

1 b	2 c	3 d
4 a	5 b	6 c
7 a	8 b	9 c
10 d	11 b	12 d
13 c	14 d	15 a
16 b	17 d	18 d
19 c	20 d	

정답 및 해설